PALMISTRY

PALMISTRY

GEDDES & GROSSET

This edition published 2000 by Geddes & Grosset, an
imprint of Children's Leisure Products Limited

© 1995 Children's Leisure Products Limited, David Dale
House, New Lanark ML11 9DJ, Scotland

ISBN 1 85534 297 9

Printed and bound in the UK

Contents

Introduction

Palmistry ranks among the most ancient forms of learning and knowledge. Some palmists justify its study by a text from the Book of Job (Job 37:7 – 'He sealeth up the hand of every man; that all men may know his work'), but it is known to have been understood in Egypt and, farther back still, among the Hindus.

The art of palmistry takes its place as a serious study in which the deductions are as reliable, if the student can be earnest and intelligent, as those of any other system founded on ordered knowledge.

In this book you will find the art of palmistry reduced to its clearest and simplest form.

The face

Whether we like to think so or not, in our first impression of someone at least, we all tend to judge a person's face to be an index of their character, and from its form and expression make assumptions about the qualities of its owner. Painters and sculptors pay enormous attention to the faithful rendering of the faces of their subjects, the best examples being those that truly show a personality behind the artistry. There are also those who claim that certain physical characteristics of the face point to certain emotional and intellectual characteristics in the personality.

The hand

Our language has many metaphors involving the hand: to have 'an iron fist' is to be ruthless, 'to show one's hand' is to reveal one's true intentions, to be 'hand in glove' is to have a very close association with another person, to have 'a free hand' is to have freedom to do something. To a great extent the personal qualities of the hand have also been recognized, the expressions 'a useful hand', 'an artistic hand', and so forth, being commonly heard. But too often hands are neglected, and even eminent painters and sculptors frequently give unreal, characterless hands to their subjects.

Fingertips

There are an infinite variety of papillary ridges on the fingertips, and their arrangement is used as a means of identification. An impression of the fingertips, i.e. the process of fingerprinting, is very often used by the forensic division of the police for this purpose because each person's fingerprints have the property of being unique.

Variety in hands

What is true of the part is, in this case, true of the whole, as the marking of the hands generally presents just as great a variety as the marking of the fingertips, no two hands being alike in this way. This is easily seen in living hands and is well shown in the nature-printed plates in this volume.

How hands vary

But the markings of the hands are not the only difference – colour, size, shape and relative bulk of parts also vary. All these qualities and the lines have a certain connection, and one observer dealing only with the outline, and another dealing only with the lines, will discover many things in common. Of course, the observer who deals with all these differences will observe most.

Hand lore

From the earliest ages of which we have record, there have been some people who have paid great attention to the hands and by much study have learned not only to judge the character but to read past events, and even to profess to be able to foretell the future. In recent years there has been a great revival of the study. Different writers have compared readings, and these readings have been verified in large numbers of hands, so that year by year the results are becoming more exact.

Interdependence of parts

To understand why hands vary so much, it is important to know something about their structure and to remember that all parts of the body are interdependent, as, owing to nervous connection, one part cannot be affected without influencing to a greater or lesser degree one or more other parts.

Bony framework

The framework of the hand is the bony skeleton, the appearance of which is now familiar because of radiography. The framework regulates in great part the size of the hand. The eight small bones of the wrist are arranged in two rows; from these start the five metacarpal bones, which form the palm of the hand (as far as the first knuckles), one supporting the thumb, and one supporting each of the fingers. Each finger contains three phalanges, the last being widened out to form a support for the nail. These are named by anatomists, 'first', 'second', and 'third', from the palm down (however, palmists have reversed this order, calling the nail-bearing phalange the first). The thumb is attached to a short metacarpal, which is much more freely movable than the others, and has only two phalanges.

The joints

These bones are joined together by capsules surrounding the joints, by ligaments strengthening the capsules, and by the tendons which pass over the joints. Sometimes the joints have very little movement, but in all the phalanges, and in the metacarpal bone of the thumb, there is free movement.

The muscles

The muscles or flesh, and the tendons form a considerable part of the bulk of the hand. Some of these tendons come from the muscles of the forearm. The muscles of the palm are those which run to the fingers, forming the 'mounts' at the base of each finger and rather inclining to the little finger side, and the large mass forming the ball of the thumb. These muscles assist the thumb to perform its varied movements, the smaller mass of muscles running along the opposite edge of the hand to the little finger.

Seat of the lines

To understand the lines on the hand, the structure and function of the skin of the hand must be first understood.

The skin

The skin consists of two layers. The deeper is the dermis or true skin. It contains a large number of nerves and blood vessels, and is joined to the structures below by connective tissue containing fat in the meshes, while above, it is protected by the upper scaly layer of the skin – the epidermis.

Papillary ridges

The organs of touch are contained in papillae. These papillae are very numerous in the palm of the hand and on the palm surface of the fingers, there being on the fingertips about 370 to the square centimetre (2400 to the square inch). They are arranged in rows and so form ridges. These ridges are notched by short transverse furrows into which the ducts of the sweat glands open. The epidermis covers these papillae, being thicker over the hollows than over the summits of the ridges. The papillae do not show as plainly on the surface of the epidermis as they do on the true skin when the epidermis has been removed, as in the case of blisters. They can, however, be seen easily through a magnifying glass, and it is the papillary ridges that give rise to the peculiarly fine markings shown on the fingertips.

Nerves of the papillae

In most of the papillae are tactile corpuscles. These are the true organs of touch, and delicacy of touch depends to a large extent on their number. Each tactile corpuscle contains a filament of nerve and is freely supplied with blood vessels. Each nerve communicates directly with the brain, and the size of small objects is estimated through touch by the number of tactile corpuscles which send impressions along their special nerve paths to the brain.

The lines

The lines on the hand must not be confused with the papillary markings. They are spaces where the papillae are wanting, and where the surface of the epidermis is comparatively smooth, flat and depressed.

Fold lines

The larger lines correspond to folds and vary in position with the varying bulk of the muscles. By contracting the hands in different ways, the coincidence of these lines with the folds can be seen.

Other lines

There are, however, numerous lines that cannot be turned into folds by any contraction of muscles. Their existence must be the result of some other cause. It is at this point that we must look at their connection with the nervous system.

Nerve action

During the course of an illness in which the nervous system is affected, crowds of new lines will develop, of which, when health is restored, some may disappear. Similarly, in mental illness many crossing and interlocking fine lines may appear (*see* A Mad Subject, page 239).

You may well be sceptical, but think of how a physical or mental illness can alter a person's appearance. A physical illness might change the appearance of a person's skin and leave a lasting effect. Lines might develop through the influence of nerves, if it is remembered that the crowds of nerves going to the papillae are each in separate communication with the brain. Undue excitation of some of these nerves may cause extra growth of tissue in the papillae, or in their neighbourhood, or, if the action is too strong, may lead to wasting of the papillae.

These nervous changes also affect the development of the neighbouring tissues and may cause deposition or absorption of fat, etc. Such changes as these may separate the papillary ridges and papillae, causing lines to appear, or may bring papillae together, causing the disappearance of lines.

Hand to brain and vice versa

Why certain lines should always be associated with certain conditions is a question that has long aroused speculation. This can be answered by looking at the physiological connection between brain and body. There is a direct link between parts of the brain with portions of the hand. The *cerebral cortex*, the outer layer of the brain, which is crucial for complex mental processes such as thinking, memory and voluntary action, receives messages from our senses and gives out motor commands to the various muscles in our bodies. A region in the frontal lobe known as the *motor projection area* controls movement. Experiments have been carried out on animal and human subjects, under local anaesthetic, where parts of this area were electrically stimulated, giving a concurrent reaction in a specific part of the body. The portion allocated to the hands and fingers is proportionally very large because these are capable of such complex movements and coordination.

The palmist's view has always been that there is a connection between the lines on the hand and certain traits or conditions of personality. Perhaps it is possible that the correlation between brain and motor function is reflected in the alleged link between palm and personality?

Future tendencies

There is one other point of great interest that can be dealt with only briefly here. Palmists of the highest standing claim that it has been shown over and over again that coming events are revealed on the hand. This is beyond the domain of the anatomist, physiologist and psychologist. To a certain extent future tendencies could be diagnosed from symptoms showing themselves in the hand. For example, a physician, seeing a patient with bluish coloured fingertips, may fear heart disease.

Many predictions of palmists cannot, however, be explained in this way, and the most reasonable suggestion made is that we have a sense so little used that it is generally unrecognized – the sense that deals with the future. This sense is seen in the lower animals, and helps to account for hibernation, migration, etc. Country people traditionally foretold the quality of the weather and of the seasons from observing the actions of animals. In human beings this sense is occasionally manifested in the form of forebodings and dreams. It is suggested that in man the use of reason has supplanted this power; but that it is not gone, only dormant, and that it may be through its automatic and unconscious action that future events are able to influence the nerve centres, and through them mark the hand.

The Ancient Art of Palmistry

While the ancient subject of palmistry amply repays more profound study by those who wish to devote themselves to it, it is possible to read any hand thoroughly, to tell the character, the weak points, and the actual events from the beginning to the end of life, from a knowledge of the principles and practice as described.

Whether it be palmistry, however, or any of the other various methods of forecasting events, telling fortunes or reading character, the chief point to strike us is the age of all these methods. With practically no modification, they have been handed down to us through the generations. They do not change with the march of time, and their very antiquity should bring them veneration and respect.

Many of the superstitions in particular are not confined to our own land but prevail in many other countries. In the Middle Ages palmistry, or *chiromancy* as it was then called, was numbered among the forbidden black arts.

The Anatomy of
the Hand

The human hand is made up of the metacarpal bones and the phalangeal bones. Between the hand and the bones of the forearm – the radius and ulna – are the eight carpal bones of the wrist, in two rows. Between the carpal bones and the fingers and thumb come the metacarpals. These are similar to the phalangeals, or finger bones, in shape but are longer. They are contained in the muscular envelope of the palm. Jointed to the metacarpals at the knuckles are the bones of the phalanges in three rows, the bones tapering towards the fingertips.

The thumb has only two phalangeal bones and these, like its metacarpal, are shorter than those of the fingers. The metacarpal of the thumb is capable of free movement, and it is this characteristic that makes the thumb an 'opposable' digit. Because of this we are able to grasp objects and use our hands in such complex operations as sewing, writing, drawing and working with tools. There are twenty-seven bones in the hand and wrist – eight carpals, five metacarpals and fourteen phalangeal bones.

One result of the great flexibility of the hand is that its palmar surface is thickly padded in between the lines of flexion, or bending, while at these lines the skin is bound down to the tendons that move the digits, and to the deeper layers. This combination of loose and firm surfaces gives the necessary steadiness and adaptability to the grasp. It is obvious that if the padding of the palm were loose and free to slip about, a firm grasp would be impossible.

The 'bracelet' lines at the wrist have a similar origin. The *monticuli* – prominences that we see at the base of the thumb and fingers – are composed of muscle tissue. So too are those on the phalanges. Nature has endowed the hand with the characteristics of flexibility and firmness, and has cushioned the palm against shocks that would otherwise injure its framework.

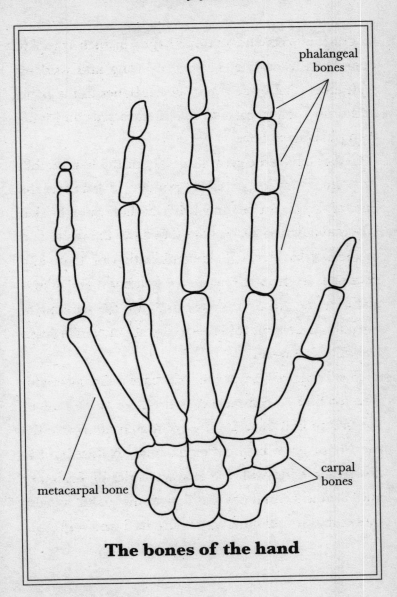

phalangeal
bones

metacarpal bone

carpal
bones

The bones of the hand

The Bones of the Hand

The Size and Shape
of the Hands

Large hands

These show order, method, obedience and detail.

Small hands

These show energy, government, ability to rule and executive power.

Medium-sized hands

These indicate a character with a capacity for turning his or her hand to anything. When the fingers are exactly as long as the palm, they belong to people who are successful in business but not in any highly specialized kind of business. Note that this hand belongs also to the 'Jack-of-all-trades' – the person who does many things capably but none of them exceedingly well.

Hands with palms long in comparison to the length of the fingers, show an ability to make big plans, a quick grasp of things and a dislike of detail.

Hands with the fingers relatively much longer than the palm cannot plan but they can 'finish' everything they do. A person with hands like these will not neglect the slightest detail. They are the 'slow-but-sure' people.

Wide hands

These indicate kindness and sympathy – someone who is able to see and consider the other side as well as his or her own point of view.

Narrow hands

These belong to people who are critical and exacting by nature – those who see one's faults rather than one's good qualities. It is said that the best husbands and wives are not found with this kind of hand, but if the life partner's hand is too short and too wide, fate may draw them together.

Hands wide open with fingers well apart

These show originality, initiative and courage.

Hands with fingers close together

These show convention, fear of consequences and cowardice.

White hands

These show a selfish nature.

Red hands

These show passionate feeling, anger and energy.

Hands of warmish pink

These show a warm heart.

Soft hands

These indicate laziness, which may coexist with distinct and probably unused talent. But, hands that are only moderately soft, or soft on the mounts, may belong to people who work best in short bursts only.

Very hard hands

These demonstrate energy and the love of work for its own sake. These are people who should ask themselves what it is that they want out of life and then set out to get it, cultivating mental disciplines so that they do not waste their nervous energy too extravagantly.

Square hands

These show reason, consistency, common sense and accuracy.

Pointed hands

These show spirituality and idealism.

Hard, square hands

Note that a hard and very square hand belongs to a person who always has reason on his or her side. He or she is never wrong.

'Peaky' hands

The extremely 'peaky' hand – especially if it lacks 'grip' and feels unreal when it is grasped – belongs to the dreamer, the impractical person. With very pointed fingertips, these hands will have no sense of reality – they will take up and support the wildest notions. Tapering fingertips show a lack of executive power.

Palmists have, over many years, defined seven well-marked types of hands:

The elemental hand
The spatulate or active hand
The conical or temperamental hand
The square or utilitarian hand
The knotty or philosophic hand

The pointed or idealistic hand
The mixed hand

The elemental hand

This hand is the mark of primitive races; it is characteristic of peoples, such as the Laplanders, who inhabit
Polar regions, and was also a feature of the Tartar and
Slav races. The palm is large, and the fingers short and
thick. It is intrinsically the hand of the peasant or serf
of times long past, it is seen in all lands among those
who for generations have come from the stock that fur-
nishes the 'hewers of wood and drawers of water'.
These people have, in the course of centuries, evolved
as a type who has adapted to making a living by hard
and rough labour; their acquisitive and self-preserva-
tive faculties have developed to predominance.

What significance is to be attached to the possession
of an elemental hand in our subject? It depends, of
course, on the degree of relation to the archetype, for
the pure elemental is uncommon outside those regions
that have been mentioned.

Superstitious, narrow-minded and unintellectual,
this type has nevertheless produced, on occasion, great

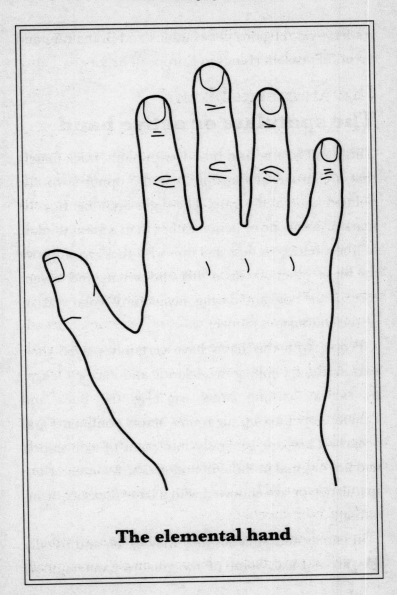

The elemental hand

leaders – in religious persecutions and in the rare and dreadful peasant risings in European history.

The spatulate or active hand

This hand is large and broad, with blunt, thick fingers that are broad at the tips. It is the opposite of the pointed hand and is rare. The digits are long. It is the mark of someone of action rather than a great thinker, of the tireless, restless agitator who seeks to improve the lot of others by his or her endeavours and adventure; of the bold and daring navigator of Polar seas, or of the courageous pioneer.

People with this hand have certainly played their part in history, linking the Atlantic and Pacific Oceans by railway, cutting canals such as the Suez and Panama, opening up air routes across continents and oceans. They are generally intolerant of convention and are original in thought and action. Women of the spatulate type are endowed with a large measure of intuition.

In games and athletics they may excel, and usually they are musical. Some of the greatest painters of all

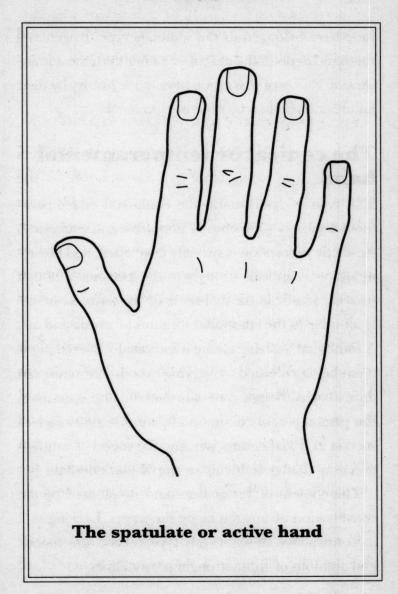

The spatulate or active hand

time have belonged to the spatulate type. In general, this hand denotes the executive rather than the administrator. Rulers of this group have made history by their failures rather than by their achievements.

The conical or temperamental hand

This type of hand marks the emotional or temperamental subject – impetuous, impulsive and exuberant. Aesthetic perception is strongly developed, and beauty in all forms appeals strongly to this person. Although scarcely artistic in the real sense of the term, he or she is sensitive to the emotional stimulus of music and art. A somewhat unstable nature is indicated – the temperament being coloured by varying moods that never endure long. Although generally cheerful and optimistic, this person is easily depressed by misfortune or lack of success in trivial enterprises, and the mood of satisfaction may change suddenly to one of black despair.

The content of his or her mind is coloured by the conversation of anyone he or she meets. Lacking skill in constructive thought, this type reflects the moods and opinions of those stronger personalities.

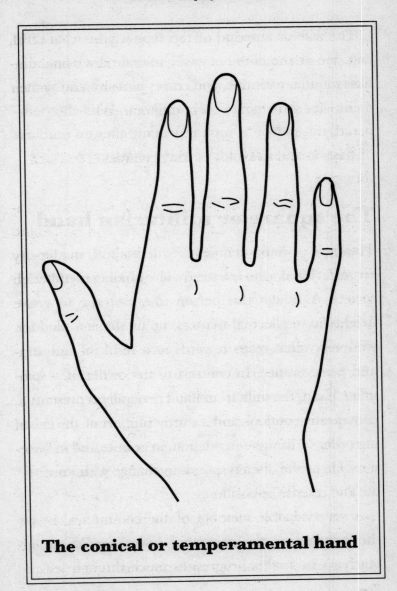

The conical or temperamental hand

The wife or husband of this type is somewhat difficult. He or she does not easily tolerate discipline, dislikes mundane routine, and craves pleasure and excitement – for something new or different. While hot-tempered, this person is soon repentant after an outburst of passion and so avoids making enemies.

The square or utilitarian hand

This type of hand denotes the methodical, matter-of-fact individual, who is a steady, law-abiding member of society. Although this person may not rise to great heights in intellectual matters, he or she is a plodder who very often reaps rewards as a result of industry and perseverance. In contrast to the owner of a spatulate hand, the utilitarian hand generally represents a conservative outlook and a sturdy support of the existing order of things – in religion, in politics and in business. He or she often responds to change with immediate and intense opposition.

A very valuable member of the community, he or she appears as the successful lawyer, politician or teacher who makes progress as much through self-re-

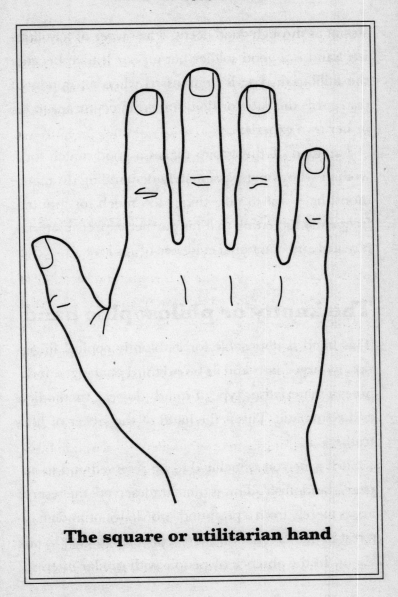

The square or utilitarian hand

straint as through good deeds. The owner of a utilitarian hand is a good soldier but a poor leader, because the utilitarian type is nonplussed when an opponent disregards the rules or does something contrary to his or her own experience.

The man of this group makes a good match for a woman who is not passionately demanding. In matrimony, he is apt to take things too much for granted, frequently forgetting that his partner expects material, physical and emotional evidence of his love.

The knotty or philosophic hand

This hand is noticeable for its bluntly conical fingertips, its large joints and its broad third phalanges. It denotes a materialistic type of mind – logical, methodical and systematic. This is the hand of the seeker of life's truths.

Such a person is inclined to be reserved and to appear 'standoffish'. This is quite undeserved; the reserve arises merely from a profound knowledge of and an interest in matters that only a few people will care to talk about. In the absence of people with similar interests,

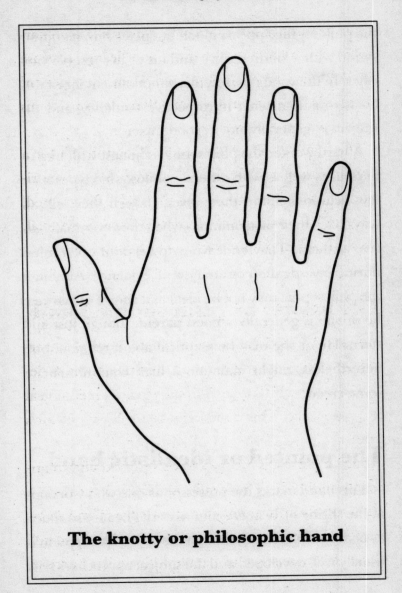

The knotty or philosophic hand

the philosophic appears aloof; but place himin conversation with a kindred spirit and his or her reserve vanishes. In the young person this temperament inevitably leads to a somewhat introspective tendency, and the subject is, generally, not a 'good mixer'.

A hard worker, the philosophic is honest with him or herself as well as with others – philosophic types have few delusions about themselves, though they will always back their own opinions when they eventually arrive at them. They endeavour to keep an open mind during investigation or analysis of evidence. Although the philosophic may not be ideal as a choice of partner, he or she is generally a good parent, though just and stern. He or she may be sceptical about religion, but, nevertheless, might maintain a firm commitment to some creed.

The pointed or idealistic hand

This hand marks the possessor as one who worships at the shrine of beauty – not material beauty so much as beauty of the mind, though the artistic perception is usually well developed and the subject appreciates true

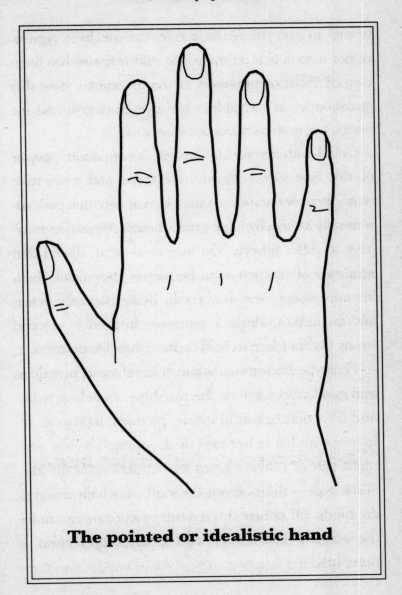

The pointed or idealistic hand

beauty in everything. As a rule, the idealistic type is rather impractical in mundane matters, and has little idea of thrift or provision for future wants – like the grasshopper in the fable, who sings during the sunny hours, but may starve in the winter of life.

Gifted with a vivid and creative imagination, people of this type love verse and literature, and frequently write, paint or compose. A marriage of two such persons is usually an ideally happy one, though the parties may have to suffer poverty. On the other hand, should the similarity of temperament be merely superficial, then intense unhappiness may result. Being naturally fickle and inconstant, idealistic types are in need of a very strong bond of love to hold them to their life partners.

This type finds much comfort in religious practices and good works. He or she worships wholeheartedly, and feels that beautiful music, pictures, lights etc, fit in best with his or her idea of devotion. The less aesthetic side of religion holds less attraction for the idealistic type – theirs is not the stuff of which martyrs are made. Of course this is a rather extreme example, the pointed type is rare, and in its completeness is rarer still.

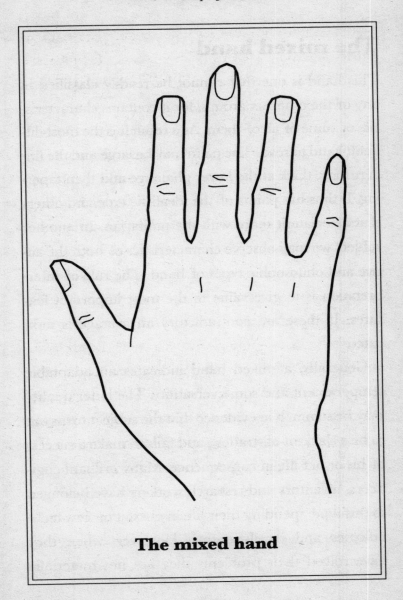

The mixed hand

The mixed hand

This hand is one that cannot be readily classified in any of the other six groups, for it contains characteristics of some of all of them. As a result it is the most difficult hand to read. The palm may be large and the fingers long, thick at the lower phalange and then tapering. It thus has points of the idealistic type and others that associate it more with the utilitarian. In another subject we may observe characteristics of both the active and philosophic types of hand. The rule of interpretation is to give value to the most important features. If these are contradictory an average is indicated.

Generally, a mixed hand indicates an adaptable temperament and some versatility. The latter quality may be so much in evidence that the subject turns out to be a 'Jack-of-all-trades', and fails to make a success of his or her life in consequence. Many brilliant engineers, inventors and research workers have belonged to this type, spending their life in pursuit of new technologies and developments. However, when they have solved their problems they are not materially

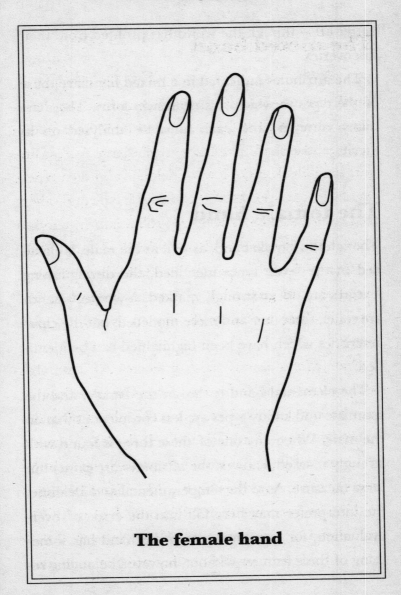

The female hand

better off – though the world has profited from their discoveries.

The attributes indicated in a mixed hand are those of the types to which it is nearest in form. There are many varieties, and each must be analysed on its merits.

The female hand

Though the female hand, as well as the male, is classified in the seven types identified, the distinguishing features are not so strongly marked. A woman's hands are softer, smoother and more modelled, but the characteristics which have been highlighted can be identified.

The elemental hand is rare in the female, and the spatulate and knotty types are less conspicuous than in the male. When any one of these three is found with strongly marked features, the attributes are present in large measure. As to the temperamental and idealistic, the interpreter may here fall into the error of over-evaluation, for in many women the hand has something of these features without, however, belonging really to either type. The square or utilitarian type is more easily recognized; and the mixed type, too, can usually be distinguished.

The Fingers and
the Mounts

The fingers

The first or index finger is the finger of **Jupiter**.

The second or middle finger is the finger of **Saturn**.

The third or wedding-ring finger is the finger of **Apollo**.

The fourth or little finger is the finger of **Mercury**.

As the fingers and their supporting mounts represent the same qualities, it is easier to simultaneously learn what the fingers and mounts stand for. However, note that an exceptionally long or large finger stands for the nobler overdevelopment of the qualities, whereas an overdevelopment of the mounts stands for their more fatalistic or baser over-expression. The hand is like the head in this respect – in the top part we read of the intellectual qualities, and at the base of the animal instincts.

Fingers that are weak or small and mounts that are quite flat, show absence of the qualities represented. Mounts that seem to be almost hollow – though this *may* be due to the very high development of the 'neighbouring' mount – indicate the qualities opposite to those for which the fingers stand.

Remember that in palmistry, as in most everything else, *excess* is not a good thing. In real life the excess of any virtue may prove a vice!

Thus, the excess of prudence is the vice of miserliness on one side, and its absence is prodigality on the other.

In interpreting the features of the fingers it is also important to take in to account their physical features. The natural bend of the fingers is important, and the palmist should be quick to notice its natural attitude before examining the interior of the hand.

Some fingers are distinguished by their independent, prominent position over the rest. When the tips are inclined to curl to the palm, a plodding, determined nature is indicated – one that does not easily relinquish a set aim or purpose because of obstacles.

The mounts

The mounts under each finger bear the same names as the fingers above them. Thus we have the mounts of **Jupiter**, **Saturn**, **Apollo** and **Mercury**, as shown in the diagram on page 59.

The mount at the base of the thumb is the mount of **Venus**, and that opposite to it on the fleshy outer base of the hand, is the mount of **Luna or the Moon**. There are, in addition, two mounts of Mars situated respectively above the mount of Venus and below the mount of Jupiter; this is **Upper Mars**. On the outer side of the hand, above the mount of the Moon and below that of the mount of Mercury, is situated **Lower Mars**.

Jupiter

Jupiter stands for veneration, worship, religion. A very

dominant first finger indicates the hands of great religious leaders and all those whose sense of honour is extremely high.

When the Jupiter finger is upright and straight, and of normal length, a just, candid nature is revealed. Should its position be in advance of the other fingers, a respect for authority is indicated. If it falls slightly behind, this indicates dependency on others and a reluctance to take the initiative and the burden of responsibility. If the finger is short this denotes ingratitude and no enthusiasm. If it is pointed it is an indication of tact, comprehension, and sympathy. A square finger is a sign of integrity, but also of someone who may be thoughtlessly frank in expressing opinions.

A wide space between Jupiter and Saturn shows unconventionality, and originality of thought and outlook.

With the mount big and out of proportion, then religious mania or enthusiasm run wild. If the mount is hard, fanaticism is indicated – if it is soft and high then the subject is said to be of sympathetic nature but with strange beliefs.

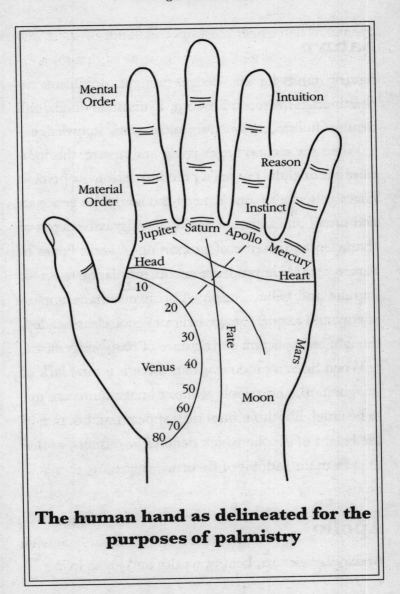

The human hand as delineated for the purposes of palmistry

Saturn

Saturn stands for knowledge, thought, occultism, superstition. This second mount, if unusually high, will denote fatalism, melancholy and esoteric knowledge.

When the second finger is big and square, this indicates a thoughtful but not a practical person – a pointed finger is a sign of unbalanced thought. The generous and broad phalanges of Saturn show gravity, depth of character, and a sense of proportion. A short finger of Saturn signifies imprudence and an inclination to act on impulse and behave rashly. A spatulate shape implies energy, and a square shape indicates cool, clear-headed, thought before action and absence of hasty judgements.

When Saturn's mount is flat, there is a total lack of imagination, and people without imagination are apt to be cruel. But this mount may appear flat, because of the height of Apollo which denotes joyousness, as distinct from the sadness of Saturn.

Apollo

Apollo signifies art, beauty, wealth and joy in living.

A long thin finger of Apollo indicates a love of colour, and if the thumb is strong there will be capacity to express this in some form of art.

If the finger of Apollo is slightly forward, the talent lies in painting, drawing, or sculpture. A pointed finger is a sign that the artistic ability is greater than the practical. A spatulate shape shows a sense of the beautiful in form and colour, and possession of dramatic powers.

The mount of Apollo is highly developed in all artists who have an inborn love of colour and of beauty. But if the hand is soft, there may be an over-strong enjoyment of pleasure through the senses. If the mount of Apollo is flat it illustrates a nature that detests joy and almost seems to dislike beauty and dread happiness.

Mercury

Mercury denotes persuasive speech, business and worldly shrewdness. If the mount is very high and the finger pointed, it indicates a person who is perhaps 'too clever' or even tricky, especially if Jupiter is poor. A crooked little finger indicates a thief, one who steals not because the person needs to steal, but because he or she likes to do so.

Mercury, set lower than the other fingers, reveals the fact that many adverse circumstances have been battled with. A pointed finger of Mercury indicates tact, discrimination and intuition. If it is square, it shows a love of scientific pursuits and good reasoning powers.

The mount of Mercury, if very flat, shows an individual with no foresight and the inability to seize a chance when it presents itself. Mercury's finger, if square at the top, shows one who can both buy and sell to advantage.

So much for the mounts that distinctly belong to the fingers.

The thumb and the mount of Venus

The possession of a thumb, a digit that can be placed in opposition to the fingers, differentiates man from all the animals except certain apes and monkeys. It is a most valuable addition, for humans could never have developed without it. The ability to make and use crude and rough tools enabled our primitive ancestors to set out on the evolutionary path that has led to our civilization of today. From rough tools man could fashion finer and more efficient ones – first of flint, then of bronze and iron – and utilize them to build and construct. No wonder the thumb is such a valuable index to character and temperament.

The characteristics of the thumb, in general, are those of the type of hand to which it belongs; but there are certain special features of the thumb that are worthy of attention. Ordinarily the thumb, when placed close to the index finger, reaches to the joint or just below it. If it does not reach this joint it is a short thumb. If it goes beyond the joint the thumb is said to be long.

The thumb has only two phalanges – the first, or topmost, one is associated with willpower and executive ability, and the second with logical perception and reasoning powers. The size of the first phalange is important in reading the hand, for if the phalange is large it denotes that other tendencies indicated by the fingers and other parts of the hand are likely to be effective. If the contrary is the case, tendencies remain dormant unless there is enough willpower to ensure that these gifts can be actively employed.

The thumb, then, is a real index to character. By the proportionate size of the two phalanges it denotes whether will or reason will have the upper hand in guiding the actions of the subject. If both phalanges are much the same in size, the individual will employ both these mental faculties equally in determining his or her way of life.

If the thumb lies close to the fingers we can say that the owner is careful with money and not too generous. A looser thumb, standing away from the hand, denotes a freer, more open nature. Then, too, we can note whether the thumb is supple at the top joint, or stiff and unyielding. In the former case we may say the subject is broad-minded, generous, tolerant and good-humoured. Moreover, he or she can readily adapt to different circumstances. In the man with the stiff-jointed thumb we should expect qualities that are almost the opposite of those just mentioned – caution, reserve, an obstinate adherence to somewhat narrow views of life and morals, and a determination to obtain what he regards as his rights. With this sign should be considered the relative sizes of the first and second phalange.

It is useful to have some standard by which to measure the relative size of the two phalanges of the thumb. Various proportions have been suggested as the normal one. It may be taken that the first, or end, phalange should be nearly half the length of the thumb, the second being slightly longer. In the left hand it is likely that the phalanges will show quite a different proportional size, when examining a left-handed subject the left hand should be taken as the representative one. Palmists sometimes describe the part of the thumb beneath the mount as the third phalange.

Sometimes the thumb is broadened and 'clubbed' at the tip, which is full and plump. This denotes a passionate, hot-tempered individual, swayed excessively by his emotions and easily roused to intense anger.

At the base of the thumb is the mount of Venus, indicating the love propensity. If well developed, it shows that the subject is swayed by his or her heart a good deal in coming to decisions. When the mount of Venus is plump and high it indicates physical energy taking the priority over emotion and thought. Those with this kind of mount are most at home working with their hands. They express their affections in physical ways and may have very strong libidos. A well developed mount of Venus also suggests that the subject may have a natural artistic flair, particularly if the mount is crossed by lines running from the life line.

The mount of Luna or the Moon

Below the line of the head and opposite the mount of Venus is the mount of the Moon, also known as Luna. When developed, this mount also signifies an individual who has energy and lots of imagination. However, if the mount is so developed that it extends down towards the wrist it may indicate that this potential creativity is hampered by oversensitivity that may be inhibiting the individual from doing better in life. Or, if a little less developed, it may just mean that the subject has a pragmatic approach to achieving his or her dreams and is not willing to risk everything for a flight of fancy no matter how imaginitive he or she is.

The upper mount of Mars

Situated between the mount of Mercury and the

Mount of the Moon, the development of this mount indicates assertiveness and the ability to fight for what the individual believes in. If it is overdeveloped then it may indicate that the individual is inclined to be overly confrontational to the point of being a bully. Someone whose upper mount of Mars in underdeveloped is unlikely to stand up for him or herself let alone anyone else.

The lower mount of Mars

Situated between the mount of Jupiter and the mount of Venus the development of this mount indicates self control and calmness under pressure. Again overdevelopment may point to the individual being a bully and underdevelopment may indicate that the subject is lacking in courage

More about the fingers

The fingers, as you will see, are divided by two knuckles or 'knots' into three divisions.

The top space, which includes the tips with the nails

at the back, is the first phalange, devoted to will, as is the top of the thumb. If this is long, fine, or pointed, there is also imagination – length indicates the will to express artistic imagination. If thick, an obstinate will. If thick and long, a strong, dominating will. But the thumb ought not to be set low on the hand if the talent is original or creative.

The middle, or second phalange belongs to reason. If this is long, then the person thinks things out and, if the hand is fairly square and capable-looking, they are able to plan ahead. Good organizers have a strong second phalange. A short space stands for those who have no use for reason. But with a clever hand, their intuition will serve them well. They will 'get there' if they trust their own perceptions, and act on their first impressions.

The third phalange, if thick and long, belongs to people of a passionate nature. But this phalange of the fingers shows the nobler aspect of the animal nature, just as that at the very base of the hand under Venus, coming as it does in the lowest part of the hand, expresses the physical side.

As for the knots that divide the phalanges, the upper knot dividing the first from the second phalange is the knot of philosophy. Large and well developed, it shows a love of accurate thinking, of exact knowledge. If small, it indicates those who are not at all philosophical; those whose acts are not ruled by their heads. Impetuous people generally have poor knots of philosophy.

The lower knot, which divides the second from the third phalange, is the knot of order. It belongs to great talkers. These are also good talkers, for we generally do well in what we enjoy doing most. People who talk well must have a well-developed sense of order, though they are seldom credited with this. Yet, without it, how could they find the right word and set it in the right place at the right moment?

In a long and narrow hand, a knot that is prominent will show a contradictory, contentious, quarrelsome person. But in a clever, short hand that is wide, indicating kindness, it means a love of debate, a talent for 'stating a case' and ability to prove things. With a crooked little finger, you might get a clever liar, if this knot is strong. But where there is sympathy (a wide hand), and a thumb set low (talent), and good head and heart lines, these talkers generally turn their charming talent to their own advantage.

The Fingernails

The nails are developed from skin tissues, and so partake of the intimate nature of the flesh. The nails may still show signs of ancestry. Then, too, the nails show signs of disease, for example, becoming brittle if blood circulation is poor. It is common knowledge that in some cases of poisoning the harmful substance may show its presence when the nails are subjected to chemical examination.

Long nails denote a calm, phlegmatic temperament – short ones suggest a more impetuous nature. When the fingernails are well formed, with good crescents and a rounded, shapely base, we may expect an equable nature and sound judgement. A broad and curved top, associated with the last-named characteristics, denotes an open, generous and frank mind. Narrow, elongated nails are found on people of somewhat delicate constitution, and are often pale and bloodless or even bluish in colour. When unaccompanied by any signs of ill health, the long and moderately narrow nail suggests a refined and idealistic or psychic type of individual. Nails with a spatulate end, especially when broad in proportion to their length, denote pugnacity. When the nails show a reddish colouring, this attribute is strengthened.

In general, the nails should be pinkish to reddish in hue, and not pale or bluish. Ridged or grooved nails suggest a naturally nervous temperament, though this sign may denote nothing more than an alert and sensitive mind. Any irregularities in the shape, form, or colouring of the nails are signs of health defects. Blueness that persists is a sign of some defect of the circulatory system. The nails are of secondary importance to the fingers as an index to character, though they may afford useful indications to health and temperament.

The Lines of
the Hand

The **line of life** (A) runs around the base of the mount of Venus.

The **line of head** (B) runs across the centre of the hand, starting under the mount of Jupiter.

The **line of heart** (C) runs across the upper part of the palm directly under the mounts.

The **line of fate** (D) (or **line of destiny**) is one of the two most important lines on the hand, the other being the line of life. It runs from low down on the hand straight through the centre, up towards the finger of Saturn.

The **line of fortune** (E) (or the **line of Apollo** or the

Sun) also runs up the hand towards the finger of Apollo, or the ring finger.

The **line of intuition** (F) is rare in its perfect form. It is a semicircle, a longish semicircle or oval line running round, or partly round the mount of the Moon.

The **girdle of Venus** (G) is rare. When found, it is above the heart line, a small semicircular mark around, or partly around the two middle mounts of Jupiter and Saturn.

The **line of Mars** (H) is a smaller semicircle sometimes found within the line of life.

The **line of health** (J) (or the line of Mercury) on which business affairs is also read, is a third line running up the hand, but somewhat transversely, towards the finger of Mercury.

Lines of affection (K) (also known as marriage lines) come from the outer edge of the hand on the mount of Mercury, above the line of health (or Mercury) and

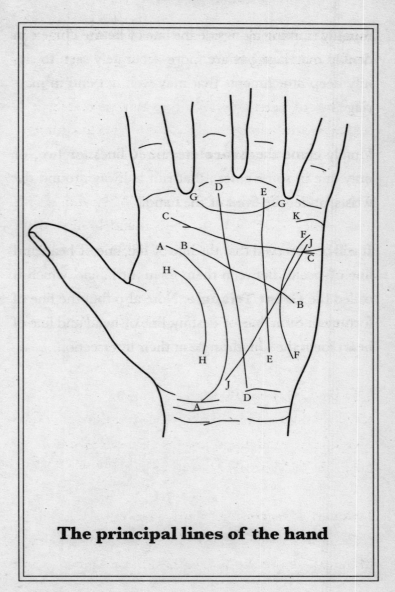

The principal lines of the hand

roughly running alongside the line of heart. These can denote marriage but are more accurately seen to signify deep attachments that may well not end in marriage.

Finally come the **bracelets**, three lines (or two, or only one in some cases), that run halfway around the wrists, under the front of the hand.

It will be observed that the line of life, line of head and line of health between them form a triangle, which is called the **Great Triangle**. Note also that the line of fortune or Sun, line of destiny, line of head and line of heart form the Quadrangle at their intersection.

Age and Time
Calculations

Time is calculated on these lines of the hands, as you will see by looking at the diagram on page 79. We have one hundred years to be read on the line of life at its fullest and longest – that is, when it actually goes round and almost behind the thumb base. The age at which certain events, represented by crosses, squares, triangles, and other marks will happen, can be calculated fairly accurately if the palmist remembers the following:

- the middle of the line of life stands for the fiftieth year

- the centre of the head line represents the age of thirty-five

- where the line of fate touches the head line at its centre is this same important age of thirty-five

• the age of thirty-five is read on the line of heart under the centre of the finger of Apollo. Palmistry gives the larger half of heart events, to the years before thirty-five.

In real life, as in palmistry, we 'count time by heart beats' and not by hours or years. It is a mistake to think that all hours – or years – are exactly the same length.

Doubtless the most interesting marks to be found among the minor lines of the hand, which indicate voyages, change of environment, talents and ambitions, are those that concern the attachments, love affairs, and future marriage of the subject.

These are the influence lines, which may be discerned running from mount of the Moon to the line of fate, from mount Venus to the line of life, and on the mount of Mercury. Their depth, length, and clarity depend upon the enduring nature of the sentiment involved. When crossed, barred, or cut, they demonstrate the fact that difficulties and opposition from parents, friends or relatives are to be encountered, or it may be that the influence was merely a fleeting infatuation.

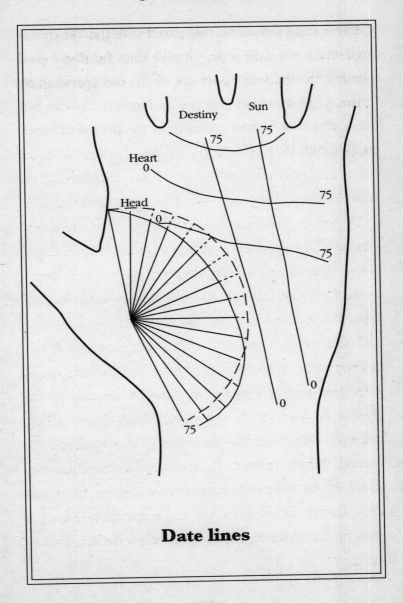

Date lines

These signs should be compared with the age calculated upon the fate line – it will then be discovered whether the influence lines are of the past, present, or future. Only constant practice and experience can aid the reader to a correct estimate of the period of these happenings.

How to Read the Lines

Date lines

The chronology used in palmistry is based upon a division of certain of the lines into year-periods. The line of heart, line of head, line of destiny, line of fortune or Sun and line of life are those chiefly used for determining ages or dates. The span of someone's life can be taken at seventy-five years for the purpose of these readings, and the lines are graduated accordingly. The line of life reads downwards, and the lines of destiny and fortune are read upwards. The lines of heart and head are read from their origin at the thumb side of the palm.

These lines can be divided into four-, six- or seven-year intervals, or as in this text, a five-year interval.

The line of life

The line of life, long, even and clear, represents a long

and healthy life. If broken in one hand, this life line tells of a serious illness. If completely broken in both hands, then life may end at that age. However, the life line may grow again and the broken lines join together, especially if more than five years lie between the date at which the hand is read and the time when the life lines in both hands end. Thus, no serious palmist would pretend to be able to tell the age at which death occurs.

Note that this life line, if chained, tells of delicacy and illness, caused by anxiety, unhappiness, or worry. If the line is red, there is a tendency to fevers. If it is purple, it shows a tendency to inherited illnesses. One often sees a faint purplish shade on part of the line of life of one hand. If in the left hand only, this shows actual illness has been avoided.

Both hands must be read, and when the life line shows a series of fine crosses set closely together, this indicates the occurrence of neuralgic pains and aches at the time indicated. If these are repeated on the line of head, then this indicates pain of a more serious nature, occurring in the head. This life line, pale or thin, tells of poor health generally during those years. But the smaller line of Mars inside the life line promises survival, and corrects or modifies indications of poor health or of short life.

Branches upwards from the line of life tell of honours or successes that are purely fortuitous. Thus, if an individual achieves high office his or her palm will show a branch upwards from the line of fate. This individual's partner, for whom this honour is fortuitous, might show a branch on the life line.

The line of head

When this line is long there is talent and a naturally good memory in the owner of the hand. But if it is too closely linked up with the beginning of the line of life (thus making only one line under the mount of Jupiter) there is a marked lack of self-confidence. If they continue as one line for over a centimetre (about one third of an inch), then this self-distrust will greatly hamper and delay the individual's success, however talented he or she may be.

The line of head starting slightly apart from the life line gives a steady self-confidence. But if the space between is very wide – seven millimetres (just over a quarter of an inch) is very wide here – this shows rash impulsiveness. Review and re-evaluation will always be advisable for these people.

The head line, if short, shows impulse, prejudice, a lack of reasoning power and a tendency to act first and think afterwards. The line of head when straight and long shows thrift and economy (with no imagination, if very straight). Long, and tending slightly downwards at the end shows sympathy and an ability to see the viewpoint of other people. If drooping low down to the base of the hand, the subject has too much imagination. If apparent in both hands, along with a weak thumb, then it may indicate mental weakness.

If the line of head is divided into a large fork at the end, one branch of which goes straight across the hand and the other turns down on to the mount of the Moon or even towards the wrist, this shows that life has two sides – the practical side, which will be efficiently conducted, and a vivid and very real life of the imagination. The hands of novelists typically show this handsome forking on the head lines.

If the head line is blurred this indicates an illness in

which there has been delirium. If it is broken in one hand, the subject may commit a serious error of judgement. A line broken in both hands, is a warning that the subject may suffer an accident where his or her head is injured in some way.

The line of heart

When this is clear and long, it gives a happy life, rich in affection. But if it misses the mount of Jupiter, rising from up between that mount and the next one (the mount of Saturn) there is coldness as regards love, with a tormenting capacity for jealousy. If this is apparent on one hand only, this tendency is kept under control admirably. Hands in which the heart line misses Jupiter do not find happiness in love. When it starts under Saturn there is coldness and a lack of feeling.

A short heart line denotes selfishness in love, where flirting takes the place of affection and may be mistaken for it. A series of very small crosses on the heart line indicates suffering through the unworthiness of those loved.

A broken heart line shows a broken engagement or similar emotional trauma. Breaks under the mount of Jupiter indicate the cause was honour; under Saturn, this indicates that the cause was a fatality, perhaps death; under Apollo, pride with some mystery. The subject does not know *why* the break came and is too proud to find out. Under the mount of Mercury, the broken heart line means that the person who was loved was thoroughly unworthy.

The girdle of Venus

The girdle of Venus used to be read as a sign of an evil life. Now, however, it is more correctly taken to mean the likelihood of some great unhappiness in relation to an emotional attachment. Its ugly aspect will have passed over by the time the subject reaches his or her thirty-fifth year.

If a man has this half-ring, he will be well advised not to marry until that age has passed, nor indeed to form any important partnerships. If a married woman is seen to have this girdle, the wise palmist will tell her to 'sit tight' until this difficult period passes. She will surely get on better with her unsatisfactory life partner *after* she has turned thirty-five. This ill-omened mark also tells of sudden death touching the life. The girdle of Venus always tells of a catastrophe that has occurred in the earlier part of the life.

The line of fate

This may start from four places:

- From the bracelets – this indicates an uncommon destiny, that may mean great happiness or misery, according to the way in which the life is lived. However, the circumstances are, as a rule, out of the subject's choice with this 'start' of the fate line.

- From the line of life – this indicates that the subject will have a good life with good chances and will make his or her own way in life.

- From the mount of the Moon – fate is made by marriage or entirely through the decisions or doings of other people.

- From the middle of the hand – a hard life, troubled and hampered by poverty or cruel circumstances.

But the line of fate that ends high up in the hand, even though it starts over high up, *does* spell success at the end. Breaks in this line are not negative, they represent changes. If the line goes on straight and clear, these may be good changes. Branches towards the Moon tell of travels; towards Jupiter, of honours and dignities earned.

Branches that rise from the outer side and touch the fate line denote affairs of the heart. Those that are clear and touch the fate lines of both hands indicate marriage at the age where they touch. A good cross on Jupiter ought to confirm this indication.

Sometimes the fate line, after starting well and low down in the hand, disappears for some years and then reappears. This means that the life is uneventful during those years. The money line also disappears sometimes. Widowhood, represented by a line from the fate line touching the heart line and ending in a cross, often brings out both the fate line and the money line again, later on in life. This only if the widow obtains control of money because of her bereavement.

Absence of the fate line does not mean anxiety. It shows that the person is only 'vegetating' when there is no fate line. Small lines across the fate line are troubles.

The line of fortune

This tells of money matters. When it drops for some time it has the same meaning as the fading of the fate line. This line, chained or blurred, tells of actual struggling, of 'hard times' due to the absence of money or to expenditure being greater than income.

A long clear line going right up to the mount of Apollo tells of riches, a successful life as regards financial fortune. If it bites into the finger, then there is a kind of 'glorious' fortune; great inheritance or a fortune received through some kind of 'luck'.

The line of business and of health

This shows the career, if indeed there is one. This line, standing out prominently and going straight up to the mount of Mercury, speaks of a successful career. Branches jutting out signify tests, adventures and experiences in new lines of work. If these last while the original line fades out, then this indicates that there will be a clear change of occupation. If forked at the top, this line shows there is great practical ability in the individual. If it is thick, this indicates a delicate old age; if it is red and thin, this shows feverish tendencies. Beware of excitement if this line looks 'angry'.

The line of intuition

The line of intuition denotes great sympathy, instinctive cleverness, intuitive judgement. Perfectly formed, this line belongs to the 'seer', the clairvoyant. Being on the mount of the Moon, it implies sadness, even unhappiness:

'For foresight is a melancholy gift
Which bares the bald and speeds the all-too swift.'

The bracelets

These tell of successful life, money, and gains in general. It is said that each of these lines, if it is clear and deep (but not too wide), indicates some thirty years of joyful living. But if one of the lines or some part of any of them is chained, there is a fight against poverty and difficult circumstances during that period of thirty years, or the part of them, that is chained.

The bracelets are read as beginning from the end under the thumb. The one nearest the hand stands for the first thirty years of life; the centre line for the period between thirty and sixty years. These are years of effort and struggle in any life that is lived in an honourable way. The lowest line represents the period between sixty and ninety years. You can understand why few hands have these three lines clear and unbroken!

Branches on any age of the lines tell of legacies. The year, in which the legacy or the various legacies are received can be accurately computed by means of the age instructions already given.

The triangle

Note that the lines of head, life and fate should form a well-defined triangle under the two middle fingers. If this triangle is weak at the junction of any two of the three lines, look for failure or disappointment affecting the destiny of the subject in connection with the qualities represented by those two lines.

Thus, if the triangle is cramped owing to the head line being joined to the life line, then a lack of self-confidence hinders success. If the head line spoils the triangle, owing to its going far down on the mount of the Moon instead of straight across the middle of the hand, a too active imagination is the enemy. With warm affections, a too imaginative head line spells jealousy!

If the life line stops short and so spoils the triangle, then life may be cut short or this may signify the hindrance of success. The fate line may be weak or poor or absent in the early part of life and sometimes spoils the shape of the triangle. In this case this sindicates that early hardships, struggles, lack of friends, etc, are likely to cause failure.

The plain of Mars

The plain of Mars is the space between the two mounts of that name. It lies between the lines of the heart and of the head, and should be clear and wide. That is, the heart line should not drop into it nor the head line rise up on to it. If it is hollow, then this plain is said to show early exile from home. If this plain is clear and well defined in the left hand, it indicates skill in chess and in strategy – in the right hand, with other indications of courage, it shows bravery with skill.

Marriage and lines of affection

Marriage is indicated by a large cross on the mount of Jupiter. The marriage line or line of affection comes up from the outer side of the hand under the mount of the little finger and crosses Mercury. The branches that rise on either side of this clear line are indicative of children. If it drops on to the line of the heart, widowhood is likely. If it crosses the heart line to the plain of Mars, this tells of a possible separation, also to be read in the lines of influence that rise on the Moon's mount and go up to the fate line. When these touch in both hands, there is a strong likelihood of marriage taking place at that age. But it is the experience of all palmists that an attachment will show as clearly, sometimes more clearly, in the hand of a single person than actual marriage in the hands of frivolous people. Even the cross is occasionally found on the mount of Jupiter in the hands of lifelong celibates, but it is blurred or marred in some way.

Reading both hands

Note that the left hand stands for the natural and the *fated* things, the right hand for what we do with them. The right hand is the hand of *free will*. If one hand is distinctly 'bad', showing a poor fate line, crossed and broken, or a badly broken line of fortune, it is better for this to be the left hand, because the right hand *may* show improvement. In this case, there will have been a brave fight and the fighter has made things better than they were originally.

If the left hand is 'good' and the right one 'bad', then this says that good health has been wasted, money prospects lost sight of, and hopeful chances thrown away. It is important never to 'tell' anything really important until you have found it to be so in both hands. Now let us study the small signs and symbols on the lines and the mounts.

Crosses

Crosses are bad when they are badly formed. A well-formed cross on Jupiter's mount stands for a good marriage. On Saturn's mount, ill-luck. When Saturn's line (the line of fate) goes up into the actual finger, ending there with a cross, there is a great and uncommon destiny, with tragedy at the ending.

A cross on the line of fate is always an obstacle, a 'check' to the fate.

A cross lying near it, but not on it, is an obstacle to a life near. Note that the line of fate that stops short in the middle of the hand indicates failure, however well it starts up.

A cross on Apollo's mount means ill luck connected with art or literature. If it is on the mount of Mercury, it shows a loss of money or ill-gotten gains. A cross on the line of intuition shows delusions while on the line of life it indicates an illness. A cross beside the line of life points to illness or trouble to some life near. A cross in the plain of Mars (in the middle of the palm under Saturn) signifies love of the occult, attraction to magic, etc.

Stars

Stars are fatalities. One on the mount of Jupiter indicates honours. On mount of Saturn, you find the signs of danger of death by violence. On the mount of Apollo, it indicates unhappy riches. On the mount of Mercury, theft or dishonour may be indicated. A star in the plain of Mars, that is, between the two mounts of Mars, signifies military glory. On the mount of the Moon, a star may be indicative of danger of drowning. A star low on the head line, points to insanity in the family – high up on the head line, it is a signal of danger of loss of sight. A star on the line of fortune signifies catastrophe.

Squares

Squares are good. They add force and strength to the qualities indicated by the mounts where they appear. But a square on the inside of the line of life, represents imprisonment or seclusion of some kind. Note the age at which the square touches the life line.

Triangles

Triangles indicate some special talent or aptitude – on Jupiter, for diplomacy; on Saturn, for magic; on

Apollo, for art or literature; on Mercury, for success (money success) in politics. A triangle on the mount of Venus tells of a prudent marriage. Triangles also represent deliverance from danger and misfortune.

Dots

Dots are sometimes of good *or* evil omen. White dots on the heart line tell of success in love. Red dots on the heart line, point to emotional love affairs. Dark dots on the head line indicate eye trouble. White dots on the head line, show success in invention, according to which mount they appear under.

Islands

Islands that are made by the line dividing and then joining up again about 1 centimetre ($^1/_2$ further on are always bad. On the life line, they tell of hereditary illness. On the heart line, an unworthy attachment is indicated. On the health line they tell of the same illness as on the life line, but, though serious, this is not fatal.

Grills

Grills or crossed lines always show obstacles. They take from the good effects of the qualities indicated by the mounts, just as squares add to these qualities. A grill on Jupiter tells of tyranny and superstition. On Saturn it denotes misfortune. On Apollo a grill indicates folly, vanity and extravagance. On Mercury it is a sign of hypocrisy, lying and theft. A grill on Mars tells of sudden death, and on the mount of Moon it signifies anxiety, discontent, sadness.

Life Studies

Examples from life

The hand portraits in this book are absolutely true impressions from actual hands. They are the hands of diverse personalities and occupations. Every outline, every line, every hill, every hollow is as it occurs on the hand. The wonderful variety in the features of the hands is at once apparent from the portraits. The significance of the variety can be learned from the text. The inquirer is advised to read the book well, carefully studying the hand portraits, and then to test the truth of the readings on living hands. If this is done carefully, the reader will learn, as all have to learn over and over again: –

'There are more things in heaven and earth than are dreamt of in our philosophy.'

The following hand portraits are chosen to show the diversity of personalities, achievements and life events that can be divined by palm reading. Some have achieved success – some have failed. Some have led and *will* lead eventful lives – some have been chosen for their monotonous existence.

To the student all are interesting – the failures as well as the successes.

I – A MATHEMATICIAN

Beginning with the outline, we notice the independence of thought in the separation of the first and second fingers, and of action – the space between the third and fourth. The fingers, on the whole, are long and knotted, and show an infinite capacity for taking pains, and with such a long head line, mastering details. The type is a singular mixture of practicality and ideality, and the perception with regard to others is wonderfully sensitive (the 'cushion' on the fingertips, and the long pointed first phalange of Mercury). A beautifully developed heart line indicates a kindly, sympathetic nature.

A love of order and accuracy is shown in the development of the second knots and the length of the fingers, while the long thumb shows great perseverance and logical powers. The somewhat slanting tip shows patience and sympathy. The wide palm indicates a love of fresh air and sports, but the slightly hollow centre shows an unaggressive nature, which, taken in connection with the relative lengths of the first and third fingers (the third on the left hand, being the longer of the two), shows his natural tendency is to have a too humble opinion of his own powers, and shun recognition. This has partly been overcome by force of circumstance and experience (the first finger of the right hand is as long as the third). The fingers are all set very evenly along the top of the palm, showing success as a whole, but not achieved without hard and continuous work (the lines of fate and fortune are well marked). His absorption in and dedication to one main area of life is shown by the generally continuous line of fate (A–A^1–A^2, right hand). There are two 'breaks,' one between the ages of twenty-nine and thirty years (A^1) and another at between the ages of thirty-one and thirty-two (A^2). The latter appears to be a fresh development, and leads to increase of money.

The finger of Mercury is especially remarkable, its length and straightness showing general ability. The pointed tip indicates tact, and the finger's length, the power of words in some special subject, as the mount

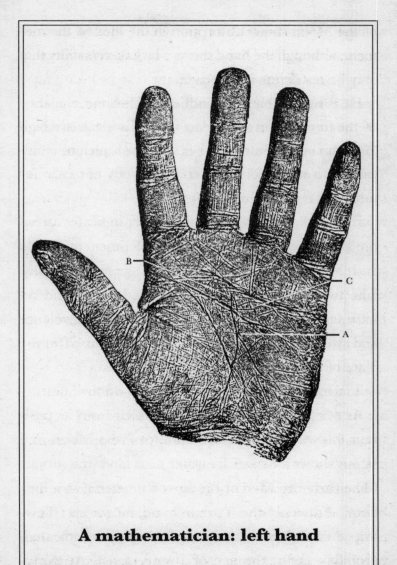

A mathematician: left hand

of the Moon shows absorption in the idea of the moment, although the hand shows a lack of versatility that may be restricting in this capacity.

He is reasonable and kindhearted (second phalange of the thumb, and long heart line). His ideals are high (broken ring of Saturn), he is very unsuspicious (conical tip to the second finger), and does not care for money (flat third phalanges).

For the mounts, the very low Jupiter indicates an entire absence of conceit, and the development of Apollo and Mercury denotes mercy and general placidity. The two Mars mounts give him endurance and reserve, and Venus and the Moon give him benevolence and sympathy because he is able to put himself in the place of another.

The following events may be traced on the lines:

At B (right hand), is a square, which from its position midway between the mount of the Moon and Venus shows a danger by water near land (the subject was nearly drowned at the age of nineteen, in a harbour). At twenty-five (C, right hand) he got his fellowship. At A, left hand, a strong friendship is indicated, probably about the age of twenty-seven. At thirty-

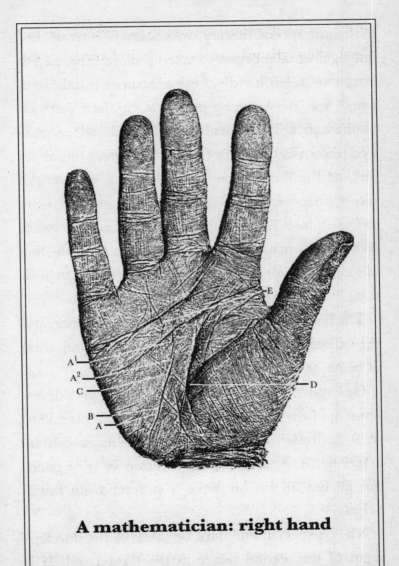

A mathematician: right hand

four some special literary work (outside interest, i.e., line against fate) began to take up more time, and at forty-one (B, left hand) a fresh enterprise is indicated, which was the bringing out of a standard work on mathematics. Two years later (D, right hand) he married (shown in the pair of prints by a small square on life), and influence line (C, left hand; E, right hand) shows improvement in position. At the age of forty the two direct lines on the Apollo mount (left hand) show two sources of revenue. Each change in the line of fate is towards Jupiter (strong improvement in position).

The lines on Mercury show the love of science, and the curious multiple crisscross of lines is an indication of being, at one period, considerably cheated.

One more thing may be noted: the square development of the second phalange of Mercury is said to show aptitude for accounts, which is a marked characteristic. The subject's constitution is very good, but he has all his life been a sufferer from headaches.

NB – A special note must be taken of the development of the second finger in the right hand. It is much longer and thicker than in the left hand, and might indicate increased appreciation of the force of circumstance.

II – A JUDGE

At first glance this man's hands are well formed and well balanced, with the straight first finger, firm long thumb, and evenly balanced second phalange, showing a cultivated nature, power of command, and intense determination that is courteously veiled.

Allowance must be made for a certain curious twisting that has apparently taken place in the casting of the hands, and the smear on the heart line beneath the Apollo mount is accidental, and must not be described as representing any special moral failure or the reverse. The main points in the outline are the independence shown in the left hand, slightly restricted in the right (the spaces between the fingers vary in the left and right hands).

The tips of the fingers of the left hand are more true to nature than those of the right hand, indicating that action is a necessity with the subject.

The first and fourth fingers are the best developed from a palmist's point of view. However, the former, although thick, is not too long, and gives him the power to rule without tyranny, but with individual force.

The thumb has a tip which betrays a great dislike ofopposition; he can be firm, but prefers settling things amicably rather than by coercion (slanting tip). The second phalange is extremely remarkable from its length, and shows the capacity for informed argument, which is corroborated by the cultivated power of words shown in the developed first phalange of Mercury. A—A (right hand), shows musical capacity and a taste for harmony rather than melody.

The lines do not present many peculiarities. Points B-B, on both hands, show his college career. D, on the left hand, dates his matrimony. C indicates a change for the better. The changes in the fate line are all towards the first finger, and we may attribute this to his general success, and yet a quiet life, towards the close of his career. The head line is one of the most remarkable lines, its length showing faculty of observation, its position (across the hand), capacity for calculation, and an appreciation of money. The different depths mark the

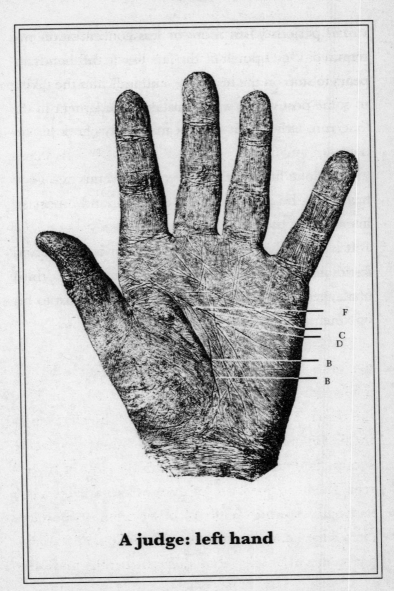

F
C
D
B
B

A judge: left hand

varied periods when more or less concentration was required. One branch of the fate line (F, left hand) appears to stop on the head line, and indicates the taking of some post which was a mistake in judgment in the long run, although it did not materially check his career.

With long fingers, fairly developed Venus and good heart line, he is patient with children, and especially interested in their development.

It is an analytical hand. Its possessor is critical and fastidious (first knot on Jupiter cut away third phalanges), difficult to convince, but always just to his opponents.

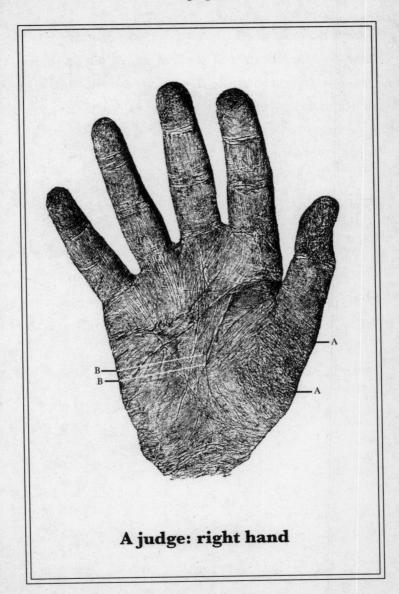

A | A | B | B

A judge: right hand

III – A CLERGYMAN

The wide, flat, firm palm and strongly marked lines show intense energy, power of resistance, a love of fresh air, and a strong constitution.

The thumb is unusually long and strong and the second phalange developed, giving him the ability to see both sides of a question, although with so sloping a head line he must (with so much energy) also be naturally impetuous. The tip curves outward signifying that he is in the main easy-going, but the large knot between it and the second phalange indicates that where principle is concerned he is as firm as he is adamant.

Notice with this the curious concentric circles on the Moon mount, and we have a character such as they made martyrs of – the idea that dominates the mind necessitating instant action.

This large mount also gives that imaginative sympathy for the troubles of others and the originality which, taken with the wide stretch between the fingers, indicates real independence.

The power of rule in the long, straight first finger, is shorter on the right hand than the left hand, and indicates that he has no love of tyranny, and not much regard for precedence as such. Should circumstances seem to require it, he can both lead and fight.

His profession being what it is, we naturally look for eloquence, but this does not appear remarkable in the hand, the little finger being rather short and the first phalange not being conspicuously long. His earnestness will make him eloquent. He will be tactful from sympathy, not from worldly wisdom. He has an intolerance for artifice and an intense belief in the power of honest work as a panacea for all ills (the spatulate fingers with the square hard palm), yet the high ideals are seldom reached. Witness the ring of Saturn slightly broken in the middle.

The second finger, while of medium size in the left hand, is curiously attenuated in the middle phalange of the right hand, but this may perhaps be more the result of the cast of the hand, and is probably the effect of the conspicuous knot between the second and third

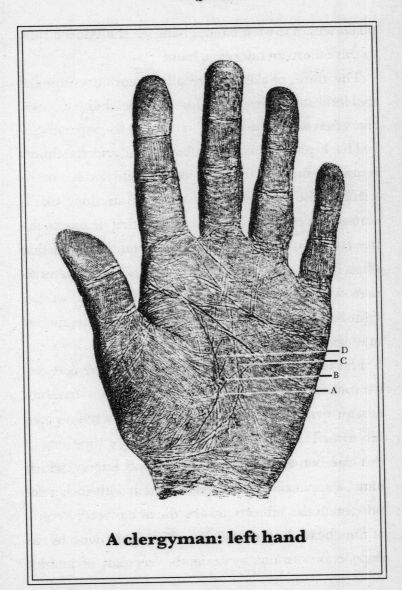

D
C
B
A

A clergyman: left hand

phalanges of the left hand, giving an analytical faculty to this otherwise uncritical hand.

The third phalanges are all somewhat cushioned and indicate a love of comfort and the ability to enjoy rest when work is done.

The heart line is particularly long and has many branches, showing that he is affectionate and has many friends. The conspicuous absence of any long marks across the percussion of Mars shows that he has no active enemies, yet the small scratches on the percussion show that at one time or another much adverse criticism was excited. Someone, however (line C of the right hand), seems to have interfered with his money matters.

The broken appearance of this heart line between the fortune line and the mount of Mercury warns him against overwork between the ages of forty-four and fifty-two. There is one curious reading for the rising of this line between the first and second fingers, which may be applicable in this case, viz, that with such a development the subjects always 'die in harness'.

The head line shows impulsive judgment by its slope, concentration by its depth, versatility of interest

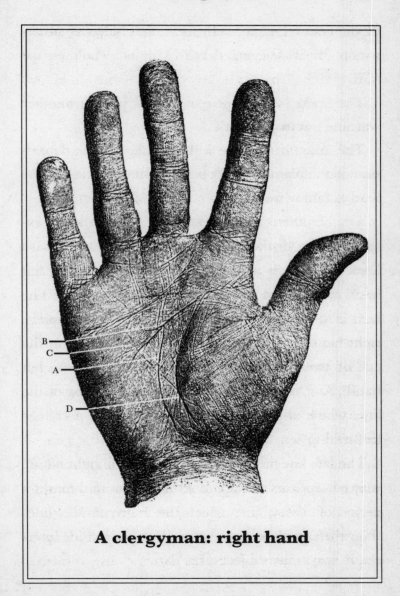

A clergyman: right hand

by the lines lying parallel with it, and 'selective observation' by its varying depth. Minute details escape
him.

The break in the centre of the left hand is another
warning not to overwork.

The union of the line with the life, and the depression of the plain of Mars beneath the life line may be
read as family trouble.

The life line is well marked, but unremarkable except for the distinct changes shown by the upward
lines, the first is at the age of twenty-three (A, left
hand and D, right hand), when he was ordained. The
next is at the age of twenty-four (B, left hand and A,
right hand), when he married and the next is at the
age of twenty-nine, when he was promoted (D, left
hand). At C, on both hands, we notice a looping of the
line, which appears to mark the taking of a college
lectureship.

The fate line just above the head line (B, right hand),
where it appears to stop, looks uncertain and marks a
period of worry, after which the many parallel lines
show the varied forms of benevolence or outside interests in which the subject takes part.

With hands such as these the subject's views will be uncompromisingly 'Protestant'.

NB – There is a curious formation to be noted in all the lines stopping near the heart line. We have noticed the same thing in the hands of those who have been prevented from taking higher office on account of the health of some member of the family. Of course, the bare reading is, 'Career stopped or arrested for emotional reasons', i.e. through the need to take care of someone else.

IV – A Professor of History

There is shyness, or rather a natural diffidence, shown by the depression where the phalanges join the palm. An absence of self-assertion or conceit is indicated in the little-developed mount of Jupiter, or the cushion beneath the first finger. A tendency to almost undue regard for the claims and assertions of others is indicated by the relative lengths of the first and third fingers, the latter being the longer (right hand). The first and second fingers stand apart, showing that this humility will be rather in expression than in fact, as his mind works independently but on acknowledged facts. The head line is practical rather than ideal, and the love of investigation shown by the development of the joints (A, A, A, A, both hands) will make him look at facts from an original standpoint. The increased thickness of the first finger of the right hand, in comparison with the same digit of the left hand, implies that the desire for power has concentrated, and (noting the capacity for expression in words shown in the long top of the little finger) he probably desires to influence a larger audience through the press and perhaps other media rather than by personal contact.

We must note the sensitive long fingers, which love minutiae and order in detail. No pains are spared to verify the smallest fact, but there is little obstinacy and a yielding affection which, with so good a head line, ought to make him a delightful companion.

His power of deduction is extraordinary, and probably as much instinctive as it is derived from logical reasoning, indicated by the long second phalange of the thumb being thick and wide. The side of the hand furthest from the thumb is sufficiently developed to make him original in his conclusions.

The lines are interesting: B, B, B, show the junction of the head and life lines, a delicate childhood, much controlled by the force of circumstances. He probably saw few people – the line C–C on the right hand, appears to cut off the social life, or restrict it to a small circle.

The head line shows extraordinary observation in some matters, but obliviousness in others; there are

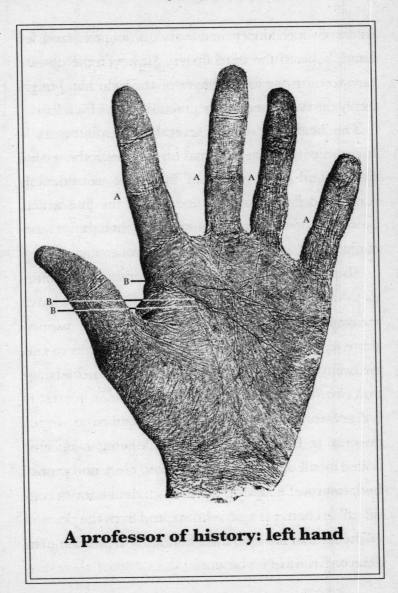

A professor of history: left hand

traces of much anxiety and overwork (looped island, left hand, beneath the third finger). However, the upward turn towards the fourth finger of the right hand might imply the capacity to make practical use of his talents.

The heart line shows several disappointments in friendship (the dropping lines on it beneath the second finger), and after the age of thirty two, considerable physical delicacy, accentuated by the life line which, however, shows that the constitution, though not especially robust, is capable of great improvement.

The fate line shows at first considerable uncertainty as to career, but at the age of twenty (D, right hand) monotonous work begins, and at the age of twenty-three (E, right hand) money and success begin to rise. At twenty-five (E, right hand), a fresh start, marriage and two years later some new enterprise or interest in literary work. At the age of thirty (F, right hand), owing possibly to interest (the fresh start being connected with a small upward influence line), fame and money both improve. At about thirty-six (G, right hand) a considerable change is again shown, and from the position of the lines in the left hand, honour and position (well deserved) reward his labours.

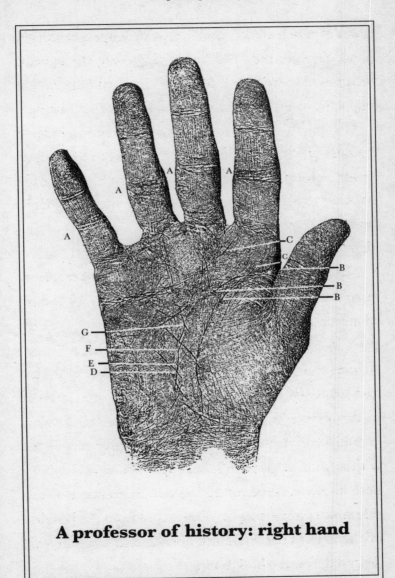

A professor of history: right hand

V – A SCHOOLTEACHER

One of the first things that would strike the most casual observer on looking at this hand is the extreme independence shown by the separated fingers. The width of the palm indicates the love of outdoor life, sports and fresh air, and the magnificent head line, long, deep, and stretching nearly across the palm, shows immense grasp (length), power of concentration (depth), and, taking the versatile talents into consideration, the capacity for achieving excellence in any subject he chooses to take up, and then, having succeeded, leaving it and taking up something else.

Taking into consideration the amount of originality shown by the great development of the mount of the Moon (A–A) and the separation of the fingers showing independence of thought (first and second), circumstances (second and third), and action (third and fourth), we read that conventionality is absolutely lacking. But having looked all round the question, and thoroughly argued the matter out (long second phalange of thumb), the subject has concluded that order and law are necessary, although the application of it is individual. Therefore, in some things, especially in his profession (a schoolteacher), he allows no one to transgress the few and absolutely necessary rules he lays down; but there is no petty tyranny, only 'discipline must be maintained'.

The first finger shows the capacity for rule carried out unflinchingly (strong thumb) but tactfully (pointed finger of Mercury), and with consideration of circumstances (tip of thumb slightly turning out).

The second finger is hardly heavy enough to balance the spirits, and a love of adventure shown in the independent long and straight line of fortune, but the inventive and imitative genius shown in the remarkable combination of the Moon and Mercury mounts, will cause him to emerge triumphantly from any difficulty. We must also notice the constructive power in the length and spatulate nature of the first phalanges, and the indifference to ordinary luxury shown in the flatness of the third, but an appreciation of good eating

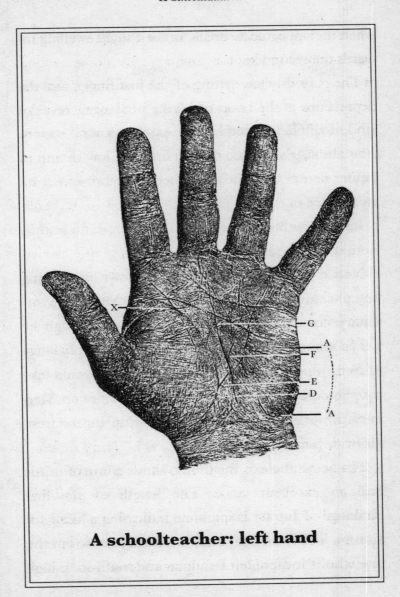

A schoolteacher: left hand

when the opportunity arises, in their slight swelling to-wards the second knot.

The curiously low setting of the first finger, and the depressions at the bases of all the phalanges, reveal a kind of diffidence and lack of ease in general society. The absolutely unforked head line and low mount of Jupiter denotes that he is inclined to be brusque from an absence of social diplomacy.

It is the outline of this hand that is most interesting, from the extreme versatility it shows.

Notice the appreciation of form shown in the long first phalange of Apollo. With so much Moon (A–A) or-dinary colour would never satisfy him, although he would immensely appreciate scenery (second phalange of Saturn), and we can understand that he would take up photography, as the love of science (lines on Mer-cury), investigation (second knots developed), and fresh air (wide palm) are all included.

The acute angle of the thumb shows a love of music and an excellent voice. The length of the first phalange of Jupiter is spatulate indicating a liking for classics. The hard flat palm, indicates intense energy, one who is incapable of fatigue and, with such high

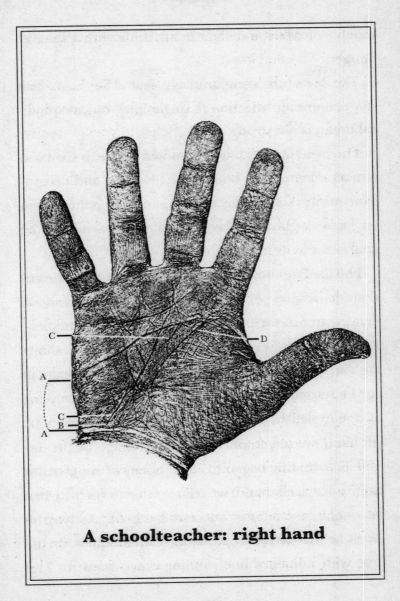

A schoolteacher: right hand

mounts of Mars, a delight in anything with a spice of danger.

The lines are comparatively few. The heart line shows domestic affection (a single line), but the physical organ is not strong.

The head line, as has been noted above, is the most remarkable one. He is an acute observer, and delights in acquiring knowledge, but is naturally sceptical (knot on Jupiter). Having taken an interest in a subject, he analyses it to its minutest detail.

The life line shows an excellent constitution; the curious depression beneath it on the plain of Mars shows that the troubles are mostly family, but not domestic.

The fate line begins very early (B, right hand), showing early independence of thought. At eight years of age he started school (C, right hand). At eighteen years of age (D, left hand) he entered college. At twenty (E, left hand) we see, from the commencement of the fortune line, that he began to earn money of his own. At twenty-six (F, left hand) we see a fresh enterprise, when he established a most successful school. At twenty-seven he married (D, right hand, a small square on life line, with influence line running down from it). The marriage made no difference to the career, and is consequently scarcely visible on the fate line. The same influence shows earlier in the left hand, x dating the commencement of the friendship. At thirty-three (G, left hand) there is a 'trouble line' crossing from Venus to the fate, when his second child died, and soon afterwards (thirty-five) a double line of the same character shows the death of two brothers within eighteen months of each other. At about thirty-two (C, right hand) we notice the development of an enterprise, and the whole hand shows ultimate success, well deserved and worked for. The line at the base of the fourth finger is caused by a ring.

This sketch may well conclude with a small anecdote characteristic of the man. Having read aloud to his boys a letter just received from an anxious mother, complaining that her boy had taken cold in consequence of a window being open in one of the classrooms, he looked up and added: 'I myself have feared that —— might take cold, for I have noticed that he is never sufficiently wrapped up – *in his lessons!*'

VI – A DOCTOR

The subject is evidently a very versatile character, and from the extraordinary development of the Moon mount right up to Mars (A–A), and the hardness of the palm, his energy and industry must be enormous, and the control of temper most unusual. His will is strong, and eminently reasonable (thumb long and good logic). He is capable of arguing out a question without temper, and is very constant to his friends (on the right hand the long third phalange B, long second phalange B^1, and first phalange B^2 which is rather inclined to taper, show a tendency to yield in small things, particularly where the emotions are concerned).

The first finger is well formed and straight. The subject is no tyrant, but can fill a position of responsibility, taken in conjunction with the long finger of Mercury, with its developed first phalange, showing the power of words and the developed imagination. He evidently writes well, and is also a good speaker, but prefers addressing an audience of comparative strangers. From the strong mark of alcohol in the left hand (X) only, his thoughts are evidently much occupied on that subject, and he probably uses his writing and public speaking talents as an advocate of temperance.

The second finger is heavy, and evidently balances the character, giving it prudence from the first phalange, a love of plants and flowers from the development of the second, and an absolute love of property, i.e., land, from the shape of the third.

The third finger has been somewhat neglected until his later years, when art and science combined probably made him take up photography, as uniting the two.

The head line in the left hand is peculiar, as the ring of Saturn (D–D) almost appears to double the heart line. The usual reading of disappointed hopes, owing to very high ideals in love and friendship, will scarcely read correctly here (the reader already knew about his marriage, as we shall see later). An alternative reading is of unhappiness caused by a woman, and being in the left hand only, it rather produced worry than actually altered the life.

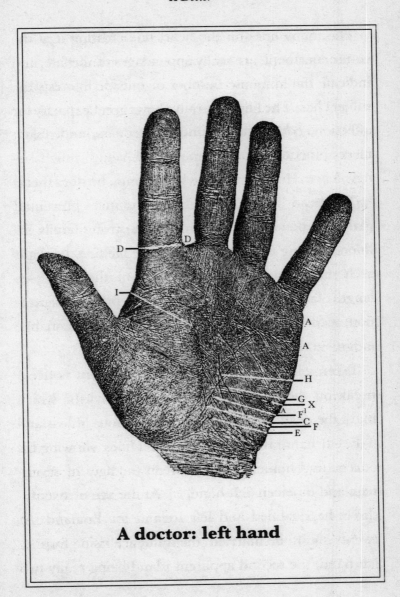

A doctor: left hand

The many lines on the heart line crossing it at the commencement, are really appendages of the fate, and indicate the immense number of outside interests the subject has. The line generally shows great capacity for affection, considerable, kind-heartedness, and, taken in conjunction with the mount of Venus, much benevolence. He not only says kind things, he does them.

The head line shows that circumstances prevented early independence, and probably a strong family influence, being much united with the life line. Its slight arch shows a tendency to delicacy of the throat; its length, faculty for observation; its depth, concentration; its downward slope, the tendency to imaginative judgment, and freedom from avarice.

Taken with the facts of the case, we must notice a break on the fate line and cross against it (E) which mark the death of his mother. The curious little island (f–f', left hand) is really two parallel lines, showing his college and home career, between the ages of seventeen and nineteen (left hand, G). At the age of twenty-three, he qualified and left Ireland for England. At twenty-six (H) he married (the influence rising from C, left hand) the second apparent island being really two

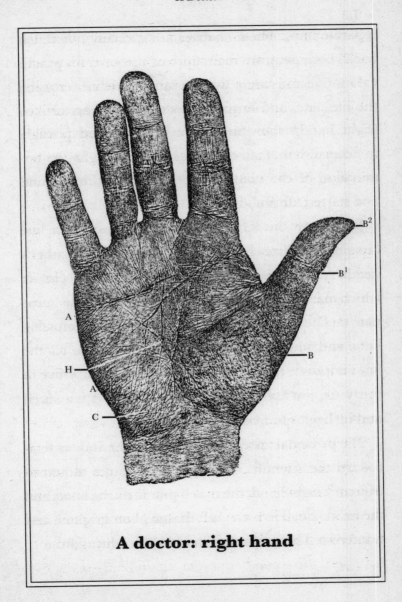

A doctor: right hand

separate lines. These changes are specially noted (left hand) because, from the nature of the case, his practical routine and career was the same. The lines crossing the life, fate, and fortune, which last appears broken (right hand), show monetary troubles, and possibly treachery, so that after the age of twenty-eight (the termination of the island) he again returned to Ireland and started afresh.

Just above the termination of the island is a line crossing the fate from Venus, marking his father's death. At thirty-two (I) on the life line we notice a break which marks a bad illness, pneumonia, and at the same date on fate, much trouble, worry, and enmity (crossing lines and uncertain line). Shortly afterwards all the lines improve, and after the age of about thirty-five to thirty-six, just above the head line, the career is assured and he begins to make money.

The principal tastes and pursuits of the subject tend toward the scientific direction (lines on the mount of Mercury, right hand, the development of the knots and the head line). He is an enthusiastic photographer, and is interested in temperance and health education.

VII – A Journalist

The typical qualities a journalist should possess are quickness of observation, good memory, facility in clothing ideas in words, and businesslike punctuality. But when, in addition to all these, by the development of the Moon mount, the imagination clothes dry matter-of-fact with poetic life, we can understand how the study before us has been successful in her chosen career.

The hand is small, smooth, little lined, and the fingers are perhaps a little longer than the palm. Consequently, large schemes will be alluring to her mind. She is impressionable (smooth skin) but not nervous in the sense of timid, as the hand shows few lines, and those that are present are well marked and clear, showing that the mind has the power of concentration, and while each step is the result of much thought, it is the main issues which occupy, attention. It seems curious that so practical an individual should yet be gifted with clairvoyant faculties, but such is the case, as evidenced by the development of the Moon mount, and the *croix mystique* (developed in the left hand, which also has the line of presentiment much more marked).

Taking the fingers in the usual order, we notice the dominance of the first, which, taken into consideration with the straight finger of Mercury, with its well-formed top phalange, gives her the power of words, and this leads to expression in writing, the motive being the ability to lead others by the expression of opinion. She can write on almost any subject that is not tedious – the small hand generally disliking any monotonous work. The activity of the hand shown by the spatulate fingers will prompt her to movement and to observation amidst her daily surroundings, rather than to the toil of the student, whose literary powers expend themselves in research. The 'dip' of the line beneath Saturn is traditionally said to show religious feeling.

There will be jealousy, as where there is so much intensity of emotion the feeling is always latent (length of line and good Venus mount), but it will not be roused

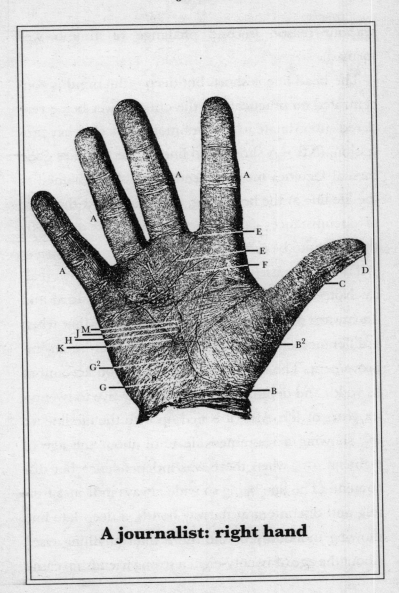

A journalist: right hand

without reason (second phalange of thumb well formed).

The head line is short, but deep – the mind is concentrated on practical life, the other power being rendered subordinate to the ambition to excel in her profession. (NB – A short head line if deep implies good mental faculties much concentrated). It is chained to the life line at the beginning, and shows how the force of circumstances caused the independence shown by the fingers to be restrained.

The life line itself appears faint, but is not so in reality. Note that all the changes shown are upward and downward (branches ascending) indicating that when a difference of life or career comes it will be an improvement. The fate line is remarkable, on account of its width and depth, for the first twenty-five to twenty-six years of life. Also, it is tied up with the life line (G, G^2), showing a restrained life until about the age of eighteen (G^2), when there was independence but discontent. (The line being so wide always indicates fretting and discontent at narrow bonds, a deep fate line showing monotony of life more than anything else.) About the age of twenty-eight a strong friendship came into the life, which starts the subject on a new career (H–K, line rising from the mount of the Moon and breaking the fate into two parts).

For nearly a year we notice a blank (J) – an accident, shown by imperfect star in the plain of Mars, which injures her health for some months and her nerves for nearly a year, so that she is unable to do much work, but soon afterwards the prospect opens very much and a new post is offered.

Also by the high mount of Jupiter, well placed and developed, we shall see that the literary gift is devoted more to the chronicling of 'society as it flies', although the power shown in the hand is really equal to more solid work and should have a wide field in fiction.

Saturn and the Moon together (the finger and mount of the former) give a tinge of melancholy, of apprehension to the character, the heaviness of the second finger being a marked characteristic. The third finger has been rather left out in the cold. In proportion it is not so well developed, the artistic faculties being appreciative rather than creative.

All the phalanges are nearly equal, and the lower knots only are developed (A–A), showing a well balanced character, a love of investigation and order in ideas.

The thumb, as usual, gives the key to the character, and here it is a little disappointing to those who expect a stronger development of the individual will. The longest phalange is the middle: she has therefore the courage of her convictions and considerable firmness in opinion. The lower phalange on the contrary (B–B), is really short indicating that she is perhaps fickle in her friendships, being impressionable and having high ideals (ring of Saturn E–E). The tip is firmer than it appears, especially towards the joint (C). Where her reason is convinced her will is strong but the conic point (D) and slight depression give, when we consider the hold imagination exercises over the emotions and the length of the heart line, a tendency to yield to friendship or to love.

The heart line shows a great capacity for affection of a self-sacrificing kind. It is long, well marked, and clear. One branch curving downwards (F, beneath the mount of Jupiter) shows a disappointment in the emotions much felt in early life.

Money and career are united in this hand, but there

will be success, as the line, although somewhat fluctuating, decidedly deepens and tends towards the first
finger. Around the age of thirty-one on the hand (M)
there is some indication of matrimony, a line from the
base of the thumb nearly touching the fate line.

VIII – A SEA CAPTAIN

The hand selected belongs to a man who at the age of fifteen went to sea, and has all his life lived near or on it. The square flat hand shows the love of outdoor life, and the development of the mount of the Moon would make him love the sea.

The comparatively small hand and short fingers will make him take in the whole of things, but dislike detail. The thick thumb with the lower phalange short (A) shows that he will see one side of a question very clearly, but not the other. The thick top indicates that he is obstinate. The straight first finger gives him a love of truth. He would scorn even prevarication.

The short second finger indicates that he is incautious, and the evenly developed first phalanges of all the fingers show him to be clever in construction The same signs on the lower phalanges give him appreciation of comfort, and plain but well-cooked food.

The fourth finger is very well developed, but not

long. There is capacity for management, but no diplomacy. The palm is very hard and gives great energy.

The Jupiter mount developed towards Venus gives pride in his belongings, but not much self-confidence. Saturn gives morbidity, and the well-rounded mount of Apollo gives him mercy and he hates to see suffering. The Mercury mount shows that he is cheerful, buoyant, and has the power of enjoyment. Its width shows a sense of humour – he should tell a good story.

The Mars mount beneath Jupiter shows that he has a great dread of physical suffering, and little endurance. The mount beneath Mercury indicates great enthusiasm and promptness – it is firm and rounded and runs into the plain.

The mount of the Moon is well developed, showing the imaginative faculty, and with the mount of Venus rounded and full, makes him romantic, and gives strong feelings.

The lines are interesting. The heart line shows extreme kindness of nature, but he loves few (deep, but almost branchless). The head line, being short but deep, signifies that his judgment is excellent in some particular matters, but he will be apt to be too much of a partisan

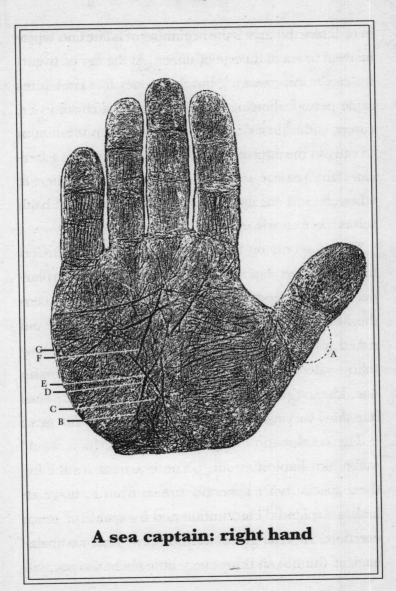

A sea captain: right hand

in ordinary things. B is the beginning of a fate line, where he went to sea at the age of fifteen. At the age of twenty his career improved (C), but the money line rises at the same period, showing anxiety. D shows a check to the career, ending in a change (but in the same profession) at E between the ages of twenty-five and twenty-six. F indicates his marriage at thirty – the one love of his life – to whom he was engaged at twenty-three. In the left hand this is more clearly marked.

One line only on the mount of Mercury. His career has always been one of hard work and anxiety, and prosperity comes slowly but surely in late life. The cross on the Mars mount (G) indicates a danger to life. He has risked his life at sea. The mount of the Moon shows many water dangers, but the hand is an impressionable one. The irregular Hepatica and the star above the head line show varying health, and one or two bad illnesses.

The combination of Jupiter and the Moon would make him liable to gout, because a man combining these special types generally suffers from it, however, he has a splendid constitution and is capable of much exertion. At rest, he is wonderfully generous (turn-back of thumb) and cares very little about money.

IX – An Inventor

In energy, intellect, and enthusiasm, this subject is in his ripest period at the age of seventy-six! He is just as ready as ever to bring all the powers of his intellect to bear upon some pet project; just as careful and exact over every detail.

We must notice, first of all, the wide, flat palm, not too high, indicating how much he enjoys fresh air and nature. The fingers (measured from the back) are nearly equal in length with the palm, so that while grasping the whole of an idea first, he can afterwards steadily arrange and settle every detail.

The thumb is heavy as a whole, the chief length being in the second phalange, which is remarkably and evenly develope. His will can be very firm, but he has a sympathetic nature, as we notice the slightly curving top phalange of the thumb, and in small matters he is not obstinate.

All the lines are well marked, few and strong, show-ing a well – used hand, a strong constitution, and a marked character.

Taking the fingers separately, we observe that the perceptions are finer, and the love of mental culture are greater now than they were in his youth, Jupiter being more pointed in the right hand than the left hand. It is, however, rather a short finger, showing that the subject shrinks from assuming responsibility, al-though he can accept it when it comes, as the phalanges are all well formed and wide.

Saturn is not a remarkable finger. There is little mor-bidity in his nature and less suspicion, some lack of caution (slightly conic tip), and a love of plants and flowers.

The third finger shows a strong taste for art, and great love of form is shown in the first phalange. The whole finger is straight and well formed, but the line that should run up to it is broken, showing that the art has not been entirely profitable so far as money is con-cerned.

The little finger is unusually good. His overall intel-lectual ability is excellent. He has literary taste, and

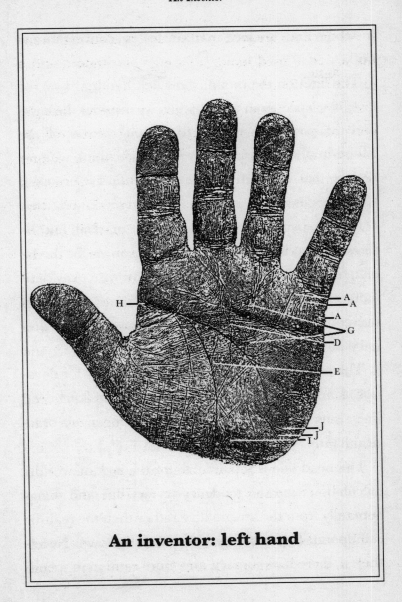

An inventor: left hand

in congenial society, demonstrates conversational skill.

The lines on the mount show (left hand, A, A, A) the love of science, from which, when we consider the knots and the power of analysis (the strong mount of the Moon implying great faculty of imagination), we may deduce that in leisure moments the mind is occupied with theories and speculations 'beyond space and time'.

His creative faculty is indeed most marked, and he shows all kinds of mechanical contrivances for the facilitating of his work, artistic and otherwise. Any difficulty only stimulates him to devise some method of overcoming it (the combination of energy, Mars, Mercury, and the Moon).

The heart line shows a very great capacity for devotion, kind-heartedness, and a desire to help (long deep line, rising towards the base of the first finger, in a practical hand).

The head line is remarkable for the lack of worldly calculation, and the tendency to view life and things generally from the imaginative rather than the realistic standpoint, as the imagination draws it down. Nevertheless, there is diplomacy, and more caution in spend-

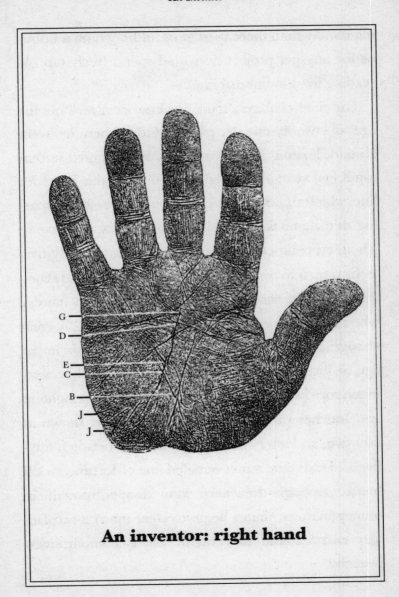

An inventor: right hand

ing money than there used to be, although on a hobby or for any pet project he would spend freely (an old reading for a long head line).

The chief changes on the fate line occur at about the age of twenty-one (B, right hand), when he went abroad, leading from C onwards an unsettled life for some few years. At B (right hand) starts the Hepatica line, which shows robust health on the whole, comparing one hand with another, except at D (left hand), when severe illness is shown about the age of forty-five.

To return to the fate. After changes, long and short, a great break occurs at twenty-eight (E, both hands), when the career is taken up in another country. A great change. He was married at twenty-eight. At about the age of forty the death of his mother causes him very much sorrow (D, right hand) as the line crosses right up and touches the heart. Another change is shown at fifty-two, and after considerable anxiety between fifty-five and sixty (the much-bungled line of fortune, G, left hand), through treachery and disappointment in money matters, things begin to clear up in a satisfactory manner and the end of life is comparatively peaceful.

We notice in boyhood a deep dent on the life line (H, left hand, perhaps more marked in the right hand) which we may connect with an angry little island (I) at the same date on the fate line. This links to when he was attacked by a dog and his shoulder was savagely mauled. Notice also the marks on the mount of the Moon at J, J (both hands), where great peril from water is shown, corresponding with an incident where the subject spent two days and nights at sea in an open boat.

The curious mount on the Moon implies concentrated imagination. The idea of the moment possesses him.

X – A Musician

The subject is a composer, performer and conductor, arranging concerts on a large scale, and never contented unless the highest talent is represented. His ideas are magnificently daring, difficulties are viewed from the wrong end of the telescope, and triumphs through a magnifying glass.

The whole hand is small for that of a man, the papillary ridges being remarkably fine, and the skin smooth and soft. From these indications we can read the desire for large schemes, wide space and great enterprises, and sensitivity and refinement.

Taking the fingers and palm separately, we noticed the length of the one and the width of the other, a singular contradiction, which combines fastidiousness with regard to small things, with a great love of fresh air. There is a combination of two distinct natures: the sensitive, caring much for the opinion of others in details, denoted by the long fingers and fine skin; and the egotistical, in the somewhat wide, thick palm. Combined with the high mount of Jupiter, giving self-esteem, we can read that although he has every confidence in his own powers, he is happier when confirmed in this opinion by others.

Music is, however, the special talent for which he is distinguished, and although the angles do not come out very well in the print, they are marked most distinctly in the individual's own palm. They are shown at A, A, in both hands, and are present in all hands with a love of music, the upper one generally indicating time, the lower, the capacity for tune.

It must especially be noted that these features mark the appreciation of music. The power of expression is shown in the firmness or otherwise to the touch of the line lying between them, the kind of music depending on the type of hand. Thus, this development, with Venus much developed, will indicate an interest and aptitude in vocal music and melody; with Saturn, church or classical music (Wagner), especially if the knots are prominent; with Jupiter, anything that is fashionable in contemporary music; with Mars, bright stirring airs,

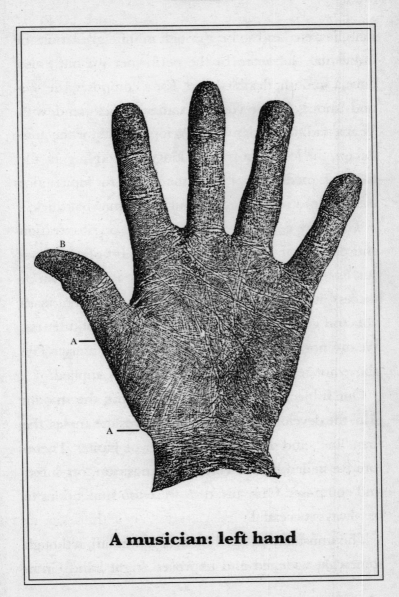

A musician: left hand

marches, etc, and so on through infinite gradations of individual character. In the performer we must also have a smooth, flexible hand. For a composer, the second 'knots'; for the vocalist, rather a thick hand, with Venus and the angles well developed; and for the conductor, the long, but not too long, knotted fingers, the palm of medium size, and the finger of Jupiter (for leadership) strong, standing out and somewhat thick.

These are general remarks, founded on observation and deduction. Contradictions may and often do occur, as it is not talent that wins the greatest renown or success; indeed, the faculty of success is a talent in itself, and generally goes with some mental obtuseness. We are not now speaking of fame but of music. The above are general rules to be individually applied.

Our subject had the angles, the knots, the smooth skin, the development of Venus towards the angles, the firm 'line', and the developed finger of Jupiter. Therefore we hailed him as conductor, musician, organizer and composer. Only his ideas were too stupendous to be always successful.

The unusually pointed Saturn (left hand), although somewhat widened and improved (right hand), indi-

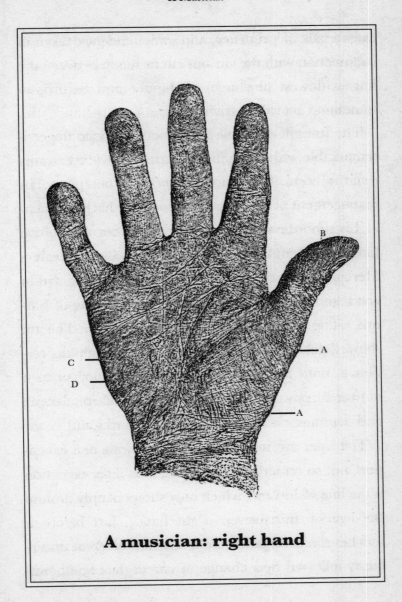

A musician: right hand

cates a lack of prudence, and some tendency, taken in conjunction with the curious cut or scoop between the fingers (lowest phalange) of Jupiter and Saturn, to sometimes act rather frivolously.

The straight and well-proportioned Apollo finger is remarkable, indicating that his artistic sense is extraordinarily keen. The fourth finger is rather poor. His management of others is not good, and his judgement of his subordinates is generally very poor. (Impulsive judgment of others' capacities and too lofty ideals – Mercury finger bent, sloping head line (L) imagination vivid, good mount of the Moon, and the ring of Saturn.) The thumb is especially remarkable. The tip shows (left hand) susceptibility to flattery (slight depression B, both hands), extravagance (tendency to turn outwards), power of argument (wide middle phalange), and constancy in the emotions (long third joint).

The lines are interesting, but are, with one exception, not so remarkable as the outline. This exception is the line of fortune, which only shows plainly around the age of thirty-seven (right hand). Just before it touches the head line there is a period of great uncertainty followed by a change of career (fate line bends towards Jupiter) in which success is ultimately great, but there will be many variations in circumstances.

The early fate line is mixed up with the life line until D, which date would be about twenty-four, when increased independence is marked.

The life line shows a delicate childhood, early troubles, and from its outward tendency towards The mount of the Moon, much of the life will be spent out of his native country. The ring of Saturn starting from between the first and second fingers, and almost barring the upper mounts, is a sign of much disappointment from too lofty ideals.

The heart line is too long and strong, the emotions are intense and absorbing. The checking of the fate line on this line shows that resulting from this tendency to excessively strong emotions he will greatly injure his career.

XI – A Singer

The characteristics of a vocalist differ in many essential points from those of an instrumentalist. The hand is, as a rule, stiffer, the fingers are often set rather close together, and the mount of Venus is much developed above and near the angles. The mount of the Moon, in the example before us, is certainly most remarkable. So much is it developed towards the mount of Mars above it as almost to appear one with it, and the plain and quadrangle are in consequence rather pinched and small. Especially this appears to be the case in the right hand. This development gives to the dreaminess of the mount of the Moon the practicality of Mars, and also an amount of personal magnetism which, taken in connection with the unusually long and heavy thumb, ought to enable him to bend others to his will. The excellently developed fourth finger gives him tact besides, and the power of imparting instruction to others.

In this hand we do not propose to take each finger in

detail, but to examine the lines chiefly – the outline being easily worked out by comparison with other examples included in this book.

The subject has an exquisite voice, but owing to a delicacy of the throat was obliged for some time to give up singing altogether, and take a long sea voyage.

Notice the curious suppression of the head line, and its mingling with the life, until A, when an arch of the line suddenly appears to strengthen, and a portion of the line, tending toward the mount of the Moon, becomes very distinct (B). The head and life are continued halfway down the hand, until starting abruptly from the life line there is a straight, short line which appears to be a part of the head line (A). This development indicates that bad health, in connection with throat troubles, arrested the career.

B shows an influence which enters the fate, at about the age of forty, and gives some impetus, causing the career to become more prosperous (the fate line turning towards Jupiter), and some improvement in money (the small line starting from the fate line towards the fortune line). Later on, the fate line appears to stop upon the heart line, and to lie in the centre of small

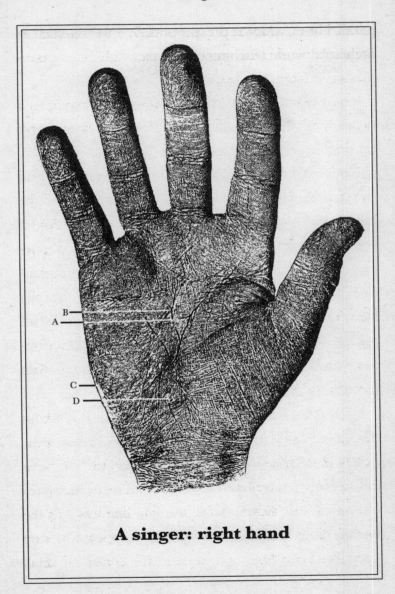

A singer: right hand

parallel lines, which represent outside interests, such as orchestral work, teaching choirs, etc.

XII – A Conjurer

The subject had always been fond of conjuring, and finally began performing professionally.

The characteristics that all such entertainers have in common are somewhat long fingers, extremely supple, a smooth fine skin, and a good mount of the Moon. To succeed, there must be both originality and imitation, and A shows how well the imagination is developed, how the idea of the moment seizes the subject, while B-B shows how well formed is the mount of Mercury under the fourth finger. Its depth gives business facility; its width, imitativeness; and its development towards the heart line, wit and humour. In combination with the long and somewhat conic tip to the fourth finger this denotes humorous repartee, and in conjunction with the extraordinary development of Mars, between the head and heart lines, readiness of resource and pluck. He is deft and neat fingered, and there is evidently great sensitiveness of touch, the papillary ridges at the ends of the fingers being remarkably high. The top phalanges of all the digits show constructive faculty, indicating that he will be ingenious at finding substitutes and inventing his own apparatus.

The lines are singular, owing to their lack of concentration. The fate line especially is not nearly so firm as the fortune or Sun line, and we notice that the fortune line rises from a kind of sister line to the fate, showing that money is made by an outside interest (x).

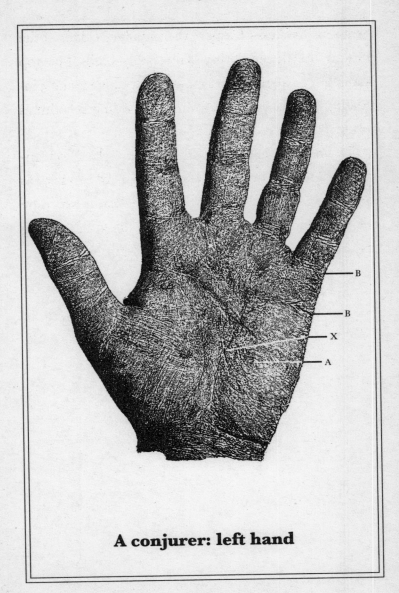

A conjurer: left hand

XIII – A Dressmaker

A glance at the subject's hand shows quiet determination, independent judgment, observation, and capacity for management both of things and people. Wherever she is, the post of leader will unhesitatingly be conceded to her from force of sheer personality, and in whatever she undertakes success is a foregone conclusion. The divided fingers indicate independence in thought and action. The high palm and Mars mounts signify pluck and endurance. The long and deep head line denotes memory and observation. The first finger indicates power of rule and the conic top phalange of the fourth finger signifies diplomacy and tact. Such a combination results in a force of personality increased by the stability of purpose shown in the long and strong thumb.

The hand is smooth, full, but firm, and the phalanges nearest the palm are all rather full. The lower part of the hand is also soft-looking, but firm, so we read the love of comfort, a delight in luxurious surroundings and every outward form of beauty. It is probably these qualities that led her to take up the class of work in which she has attained such success. In addition, the power of imitation is extremely developed, so that she can not only quickly grasp an idea, but apply it in a totally novel manner. She is in addition a good business woman (mount of Mercury developed for imitation, more towards the percussion for business), so that we are not surprised to see that money has been made and kept.

The outline shows less construction than we should imagine, but it is she who conceives, orders, and arranges, leaving the actual work to be done by others. Notice the combination showing love of rule (good first finger, good heart line and strong long thumb) and this – with imagination shown on the mount of the Moon, which gives her sympathy besides – indicates power over others, and the ruling of her subordinates kindly but with much firmness.

The mounts show more clearly in this print than in some others. Jupiter is developed towards Saturn,

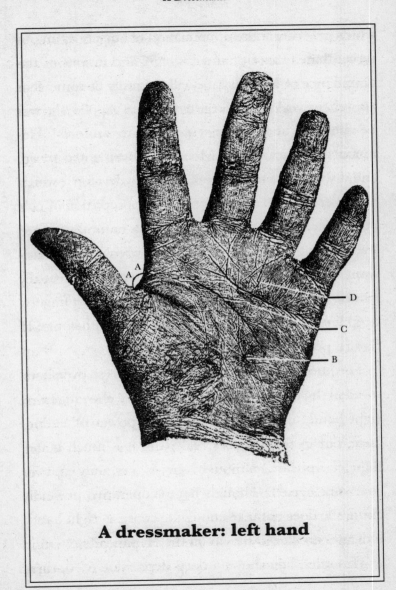

A dressmaker: left hand

which gives her more appreciation of society as an observer than a sharer; Saturn is high, and in spite of the dominance of Mercury she will naturally be somewhat apprehensive. With so large a mount of Apollo, she will be merciful and kindly, especially to animals. The mounts of Mars and the Moon have been noted above, and if we see the tendency of Venus to develop towards the outer angles we shall notice the appreciation of colour, music, melody, etc. The subject is naturally impulsive and intense, there is a love of speculation and a want of ordinary caution, but it must be a great dilemma that she cannot find a way out of (short fingers, deep lines, long finger of Apollo, and top phalange of Saturn pointed).

The lines are interesting. The life line is so overshadowed in the print by the mount of Mars, showing (A–A, right hand, and A–A, left hand) the power of endurance, but in the subject's real palm it is much better than it appears, although she is certainly apt to overwork herself. Though her recuperative power is good, she does not take enough exercise. B, right hand, indicates an illness, shown on the Hepatica line.

This same line shows a deep depression (C–C, right

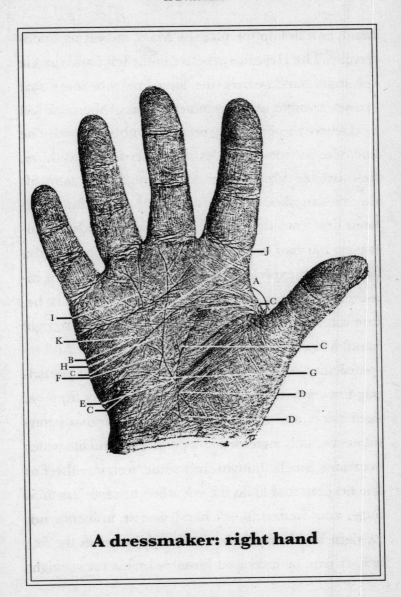

A dressmaker: right hand

hand) as it lies on the plain of Mars, indicating family trouble. The Hepatica is better in the left hand than in the right hand, where the long line that loops and crosses it might seem to indicate that at the same period where the deepest depression is noticed on the life line, viz, between the ages of twenty-four and thirty-four, trouble affected her general health. In later life there is a marked improvement. The separation of the head line from the life is most definite. Evidently the subject has had to make up her mind early, and is accustomed to expressing her opinions freely. Notice besides how clear is a short early fate line, where just before it disappears into the life line it shows (D-D, right hand) a decided line, i.e., early independence and responsibility. At E, right hand (from the ages of twenty-one to twenty-two), there is a breaking away from old association, and at twenty-six (F, right hand) a strong influence, with increased independence, and life which occasions much thought and some worry – the fate line deepens and looks frayed, a line towards the third finger rises from it (B, left hand) and an influence line (G, right hand) rises from the life and touches the fate line. A new or increased business opens between the ages of thirty-one and thirty-two (H, right hand) and a year or two afterwards, owing to bad debts, etc, there were considerable monetary troubles. Yet at the same time a curious line begins to rise (I, right hand) which seems a wandering fortune line, and yet crosses this and rises to Jupiter – it is an unusual line, and indicates position and money from the pursuit of some career. Notice also how just below the head line the fate is crossed by trouble from relatives, and between the ages of thirty-nine and forty again (C, left hand, and J, right hand) the tangling of the fortune line indicates monetary trouble. After the heart line, however, these are triumphantly survived, and the doubled line under the third finger (D, left hand, K, right hand) shows that this improvement is maintained. The fate line tends towards the Apollo side of Saturn, indicating a sociable but not society life.

The heart line shows by its length an affectionate disposition rising to a capacity for devotion. When we observe the one long deep line rising to between the first and second fingers, and that in later life the material organ is not so strong, the subject should be warned not to do too much.

XIV – A Charity Worker

We can see at a glance that the owner of these hands is at once nervous, sensitive, and yet plucky. The numberless fine lines intersecting the hand at all angles betray a susceptibility to outward influences, such as weather, while the improvement in the mount of Mars, under Jupiter, in the right hand shows how much fortitude has been increased through practice.

Mercury is evidently the dominant finger, showing an unusual talent for dealing with people, especially children and dependants – an almost passionate love of justice would cause their claims to be considered before any personal convenience (the very straight outer line of the Jupiter finger, combined with the well developed mount of Apollo). The comparatively short finger of Jupiter (right hand) contrasted with the great difference in the respective lengths of the two Apollo fingers, shows that while enterprise has increased, reverence has somewhat diminished; the 'knots' have grown and developed, and taken in conjunction with the ring of Saturn, indicated above the heart line, we may conclude that it is her high ideals which lead to disappointment, and increase the difficulty of belief in both persons and things.

Saturn is not so heavy a finger as we might expect. It just balances the romantic impulsive judgment, but only just! It is not a hand that will ever humbly bow to circumstances: it will always make a gallant struggle which in the end will force the circumstances themselves to yield.

The third finger has a remarkably developed first phalange. Indeed, all the first phalanges are long and well formed, showing good constructive power; but the finger being otherwise somewhat thin, there is no artistic career, and the love of art would rather appear in decoration, dress, and the power of appreciation.

Mercury, on the contrary, asserts itself, and, in addition to the qualities enumerated above, shows an excellent capacity for expression in words, which, taken with the mount (giving a sense of humour), would make her a most agreeable companion. This is due to

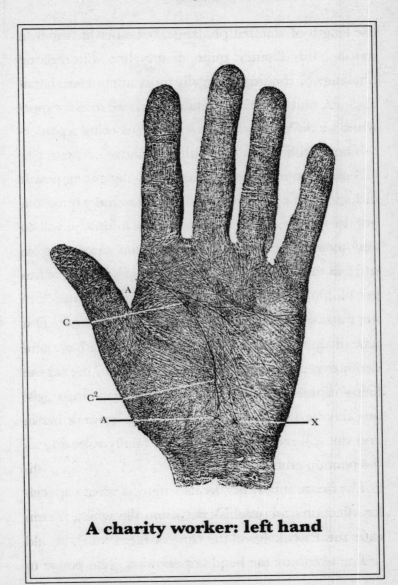

A charity worker: left hand

the length of the first phalange, but when it comes to writing, this fluency quite deserts her. The second phalange of this finger is really more attenuated than it appears, and is decidedly thin, which we might expect when we discover her intense dislike of using a pen!

The thumb shows in its third phalange constancy to all emotions; in its second, an unusually strong power of logic, or the capacity for seeing all round a question, but the first 'tails off', as it were – not a forceful will by any means, although, perhaps, often appearing as such, as the pride shown in the development of the finger of Jupiter would often lead the subject to stick to her guns, even when intensely weary of the strife. This type of thumb also indicates that the subject has a tendency to repress her anger or frustration for the sake of being diplomatic. However, a minor incident might one day be the 'straw that breaks the camel's back', and she will seemingly over-react, finally releasing all the pent up emotion.

The heart line shows, by its length, a great capacity for affection and unselfish devotion. Physically, it indicates some weakness at the close of life.

The length of the head line shows a great power of

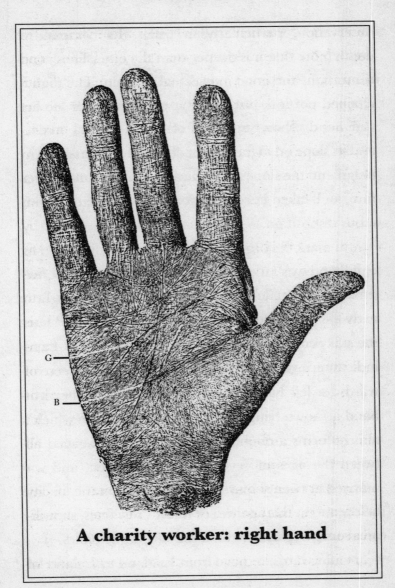

A charity worker: right hand

observation, particularly in trifles. Its comparative depth (note that it is deeper than the other lines), concentration, and good intellectual capacity. The slightly chained portion, just where it parts from the life line (left hand), shows a period of much mental anxiety, and its slope on to the mount of the Moon, imaginative judgment; the slope also indicates an uncalculating nature, and, taken in conjunction with the stretch, a generous disposition.

A, A, mark the beginning and end of the life line. Her childhood was an extremely unhappy one (a generally broken line, while the fate being good and straight in early life (X), health is not the cause of the frayed line), the star occurs at about nine years of age (right hand) indicating a great shock. From the age of seventeen onwards (C, left hand) the strong influence of her husband is shown lying close to the life line, with which it almost forms a double line. She became engaged between the ages of seventeen and eighteen, and was married at twenty-four (B, right hand). On the life line below and at this age we see many cross lines, showing great with regard to the family (G, right hand). Two years afterwards, a move from England to Ireland occurs (a break in the fate line), and there is trouble from the husband's family between the ages of twenty-six and twenty-eight. (Note a line crossing the fate, just below the doubling of the line, and inclined to island after crossing.) Many family troubles cross the fate between the head and heart lines. Small lines running parallel with the fate line show outside interests, philanthropy, etc. Money matters will show much improvement towards the middle and the end of her life.

The hand has been used as an example because the marriage shows so very clearly, and the husband's influence lasts the whole life (line inside life line, c-c^2, left hand).

XV – A Mystic

The subject is a mystic whose talents are renowned and whose life has been by no means uneventful. Her presence is impressive but not overbearing. This is a highly sensitive, gentle and impressionable woman.

An impression was made of one hand only, as she wore on the other an antique and world-famous ring, to which she feared damage; but the hand is singularly interesting, chiefly because it reveals very unexpected features.

That she has achieved what she has we may account for by the length of her fourth finger (Mercury), with its conic tip; her long and strong thumb, giving her personality, consistency, and the power of seeing all sides of a question. The capacity for rule is shown in the dominant first finger. The absence of morbidity is seen in the conic tip to Saturn, and the amount of style and panache in the straight and long Apollo finger. The hollow palm ought, according to older writers, to destroy the power of all these good qualities – but it doesn't.

It is certainly very concave, particularly beneath the life line, which is said to indicate family trouble. However, in this instance we are inclined to think that whereas a high, hard palm denotes aggressiveness, the peculiar hollowness of this would rather imply a yielding to or waiting on fate, or the tendency to be impressed, to live each moment as it comes, and not to fight against or force circumstances. To such a hand noise, combat, and strife are antagonistic. In the long heart line and remarkable head line we can perceive the force of feeling and the foresight which, having identified the need of conflict, would carry it through.

A, A, A, all show various important journeys. That they are mostly looped, implies a 'going out' and 'a return'.

On the mount of Mars, B, B, B, show three distinct attempts on the part of enemies to frustrate her plans. For these lines to mark so deeply, they must have been periods of much strife. C, the 'ring of Solomon', gives, with developed mount of the Moon, occultism.

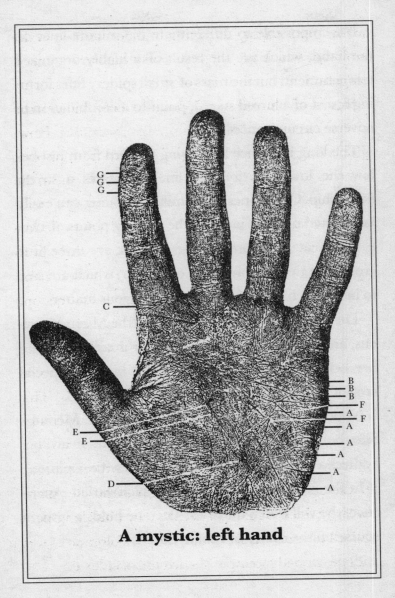

A mystic: left hand

It is impossible to differentiate the minute lines on the hand, which are the result of a highly organized temperament, but the mass of small spidery lines forming a sort of blurred star, D, point to a combination of adverse circumstances.

The long influence line, rising upward from just below the lowest A (journey line), indicates a strong friendship. Other lines of a similar character can easily be pointed out. F, F indicate the starting points of two. E, E, indicate legal proceedings. G, G, G, are three little crosses on the first phalange of Jupiter, which are said to indicate change of opinions in religious matters.

The development of the mount of the Moon is curious, and the mount is very firm. Her imagination and her occultism have been cultivated in some special area of thought.

Notice, too, the long upper phalange of Mercury. She should speak well (and anyone who has heard her address a crowded audience will endorse the opinion).

In the end, after living a life of such varied experience, she will lead a quiet life (fate line holds a straight course up the centre of mount Saturn).

XVI – A Dancer

A quiet, refined manner and a pretty face, graceful and gentle. The dancer chosen as an example began performing publicly at a very early, and worked immensely hard at her career from the age of fourteen. Like so many others, her work in life is well done, but not entirely self-chosen. The love of culture and of art, shown in the conic third finger inclining to spatulate, has had little opportunity for developing, but is probably hereditary.

The power of organization, tact, and perseverance, is shown in the first and fourth fingers and long firm thumb.

Notice how free the hand is from '*nerve*' lines; she does not brood over things. Her career is chosen, and is perhaps a little monotonous, but is evidently persevered in (fate line deep and even), and as time goes on, there is a change very much for the better to be noted.

At B a legacy runs into the fortune line, expected or anticipated for a short time before it comes; consummated in spite of opposition between the ages of forty-eight and fifty (D), causing a change for the better (C) at the same age. She is about thirty now.

There is a very well marked angle where we read 'time' (X), but there is no corresponding lower one of 'tune'. She is an excellent timist, although no musician, and her artistic tendencies show her the most effective groupings as to colour, etc.

A shows her marriage at twenty-three (an influence line running into fate and life, which starts to join in the fate line).

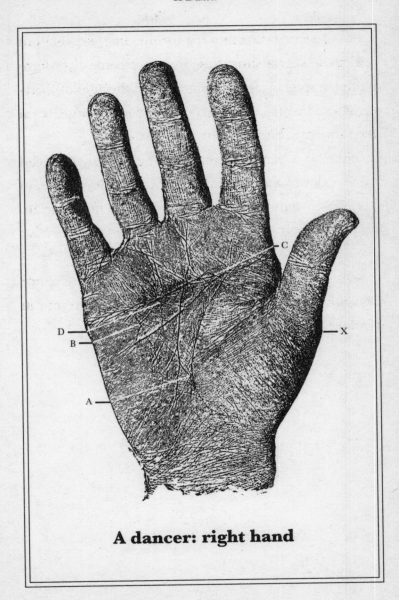

A dancer: right hand

XVII – A DISCIPLINARIAN

After reading the various striking points of character in the palm of this subject, the predominance of Mars in plain and mounts, which although not so apparent in the prints is in reality a great characteristic, caused the palm reader to remark, 'You ought to enjoy military spectacles, as order, precision and (noting the first and fourth fingers) command are very marked in your hands'. The subject laughed, and some time afterwards, when the reader met her in her own surroundings, the point of the joke was accentuated. Some hundred girls performed with the utmost military precision a series of most complicated and difficult tasks, the subject herself – apparently the most unconcerned spectator – having trained them; and although seemingly absorbed in conversation, yet not a movement or look escaped her all-comprehending eyes. One celebrated general remarked that if his soldiers were in such good order as her girls he should be content!

Order, command, organization, tact and promptness are therefore the leading characteristics of this subject, the development of the joints between the middle and lower phalanges giving her sense of order a particular characteristic in practical life.

The first finger has not come out well in the print of the right hand. It is well formed, straight and stands out in a marked manner, showing that leadership is the characteristic employment of its owner, while the long pointed top phalange of the little finger shows she has skill in maintaining discipline without causing resentment.

The thumb is long and strong. The second phalange is remarkable for its even development. The subject is not averse to argument and can see all sides of a question. The top phalange is much thicker towards the base. This is the knot which intensifies the force of will, but as the tip slightly tapers there is no obstinacy. In ordinary life the subject yields to emotion and circumstances, but where principle is concerned she is adamant!

The second finger is hardly strong enough for the rest of the naturally impulsive hand (small hand, fin-

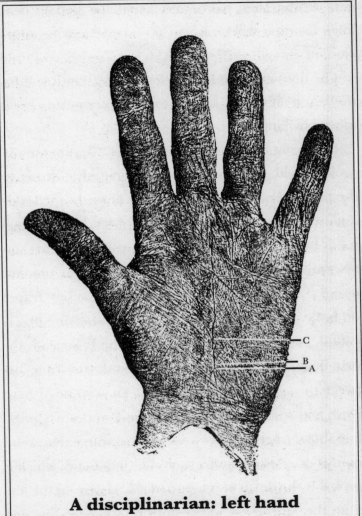

A disciplinarian: left hand

gers shorter than palm, and somewhat sloping head line). Caution will be learnt by experience, but suspicion, never.

The lines are extremely fine and the skin is soft betraying a sensitive and sympathetic nature, easily moved by kindness.

The heart line is long, showing an affectionate disposition with many branches, particularly just before the fate line passes it (right hand). These branches do not droop, but appear crossed. Her friendships are not spoilt by treachery or disappointment. The heart sorrows are caused by death. Later on in life the physical organ shows some inherited weakness (the line frayed on both hands). The head line is long showing observation. Note how deeply it is marked just beneath the first finger (A-A, right hand). Evidently the time between the ages of twelve and eighteen was one of hard work and study. Afterwards a period comes when the line shows traces of overwork and nervous exhaustion, many occupations, and a shock (B, right hand) which is probably the death of a friend (not a relative) as the line from the heart downwards stops on the head line and does not continue downwards and cross the life line. After

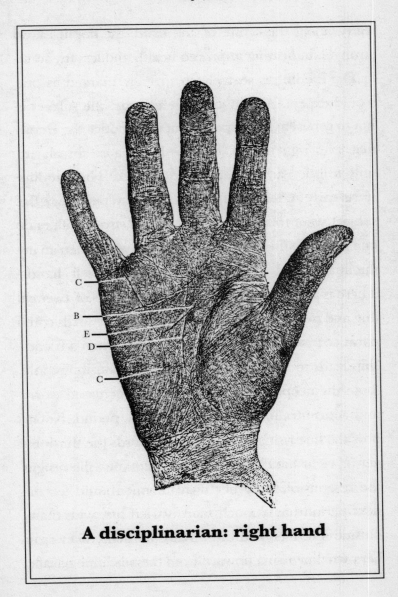

A disciplinarian: right hand

thirty, about the centre of the hand, the line is much stronger, indicating improved health and less friction.

The life line is scarcely so strongly marked as one would expect. Although very energetic, the subject is not so robust as she appears; but if we notice the Hepatica (C-C, right hand), there is little cause for alarm, only a little warning against overwork. The fate line starts early (A, left hand), when at nine years of age the subject went to school. Notice how a strong influence line rises into the career the following year, when an influential friend almost adopted her (B, left hand). There is a distinct change between the ages of twenty-one and twenty-two (C, left hand) and afterwards comparative monotony until D, right hand, when a friendship leads to matrimony. Increased responsibility, and (note the deepening of the fate line) increased worry and concentration, all mark the same period. Notice how the line rising from the fate towards the third finger (E, right hand) stops on the head line. She resigns the responsibility by her own judgment, and for the next period has a much more varied life, with many outside interests, and the threads of many lives cross her own (line rising upward from the head line parallel with the fate). The numerous cross lines from the root of the thumb towards the life show that she will all her life be a centre for many friendships, and while anxiety about money will be more or less a fact during life (fluctuating fortune line), a sunny disposition will predominate.

XVIII – Money

'Whereunto is money good?
Who has it not, lacks hardihood.
Who has it, has much trouble and care,
Who once had it, has despair.'

So sings the poet, and, however philosophically we may speak of poverty, the power of the 'almighty dollar' is no mean factor in our daily life. The special line on which the fluctuations of wealth are traced has its place generally beneath the third finger, and, like the fate line, is reckoned upwards. Its place of rising varies according to circumstances. Depth does not signify the accumulation of wealth, but generally the detailed thought given to spending small amounts, while lines running into it show increase from different sources, such as legacies, and on parallel lines are shown different interests in connection with it.

Losses of money are shown by a broken line, star, or islands, depending on whether the loss is caused by misfortune, shock, or treachery.

We must notice one peculiarity of the line, and that is its growth both upwards and downwards. Frequently a small line beneath the third finger begins to grow downwards and then a rising line develops upward, and uniting betrays that which appeared to be only a stray marking is really the fortune or Sun line. This line refers to fluctuation of money and that only on the development of this line. True, it is very often present in the hands of those who have had successful careers, but in ordinary parlance this is to make money out of one's talents, and the changes of the line would be at a period when monetary affairs were easy or otherwise, and not a special success in the talent shown to be possessed (and used) by the outline of the hand.

It cannot be too strongly emphasised that it is not the possession of money but the thought expended on the various events that really marks the hand, and when the matter of daily expenditure is the main channel of anxious thought, we see a very deeply marked 'money' line, whereas in those who spend freely out of

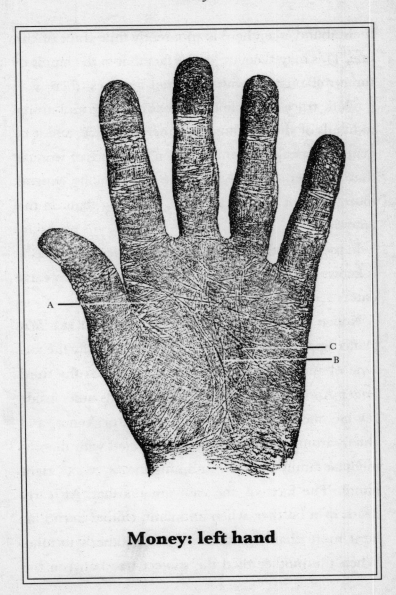

Money: left hand

their abundance, there is apparently little trace of the line. This may account for the fact that in the hands of three millionaires, with inherited fortunes, there was but little trace of this line, whereas it is deep and strong in hands of those toiling for a mere pittance, and it is, generally speaking, found more in the hands of women than of men, possibly because they usually expend more thought on the details of spending than on the amount.

In the hand selected to give an example of this line, it is known that the subject was an heiress from an early date.

Notice in the right hand that the line that at a first glance appears to be either life or fate, is really the fortune or money line, rising directly towards the third finger, Apollo. The root of this line begins quite inside the life line at the base of the mount of Venus, and chiefly from two sources, *both* connected with the immediate family (two lines running into A, X^1, X^2, right hand). The facts of the case are unusual. An early death of a brother, when an infant, caused her to inherit more than her share of her mother's fortune. When the mother died the subject was between the

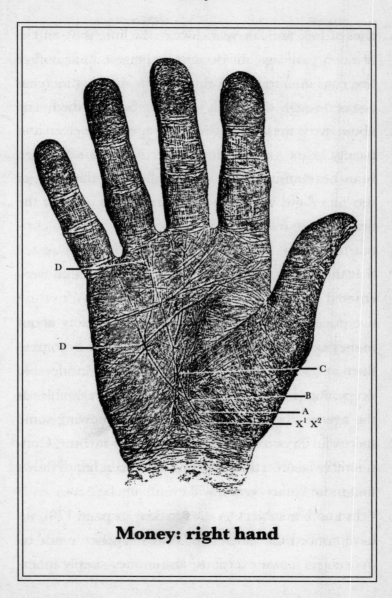

Money: right hand

ages of four and five years (where the line rises), and so at a very early age, she became an heiress. At B another line runs in, also on the thumb side, showing increase again through the family (another brother died) and about five years later, between the ages of nineteen and twenty years (C, right hand), the same line has two branches running into it, one smaller than the other, as the 'lucky' girl was left two fortunes in the year by the death of two relatives. The line waves slightly in a curious manner at this point, and (at A, left hand) we see that the reason was some legal proceedings that were entered into by the self-will of the subject. At twenty-five (B, left hand) she marries, and her anxiety about money begins to occupy the mind, the line becoming fluctuating and faint (left hand), and considerably deepening (right hand) after that period. It doubles at the age of about thirty (C, left hand), showing some successful investment, a second source of income. Considerably later on the rising line (D-D, right hand) shows that more family wealth will eventually be hers.

In another subject (A dressmaker, *see* page 179), we have noticed the difference between money made by the subject's own exertions, and money simply inherited, and in yet another (An inventor, *see* page 155) the loss of money through treachery is clearly seen.

The characteristic of the present subject is a great love of fresh air and sport. She is a fearless horse-woman (hand squared wide and flat, high mount Mars and good mount of the Moon), but it is as the possessor of wealth, and as someone who has also worried a great deal about her finances that she makes such an interesting subject for study.

XIX – MATRIMONY

The subject has a charming personality. Her principal mounts are Mars, the Moon and Apollo, Jupiter and Venus being secondaries, not much developed and rather soft. Saturn's finger is markedly long, but in her personal appearance the only trace of his influence is indicated in her black eyelashes, which shade blue eyes with the Mars shade, deepened by the influence of Apollo. Her artistic faculties are very marked, in music, vocal and instrumental, and in dramatic art, while in literature of a lighter, social kind, she could excel, the difficulty being to choose which talent would be best to cultivate. A-A mark the angles of time and tune.

In so musical a hand the Moon and Saturn mounts give the facility for composition, which must be taken with the long finger of Mercury and the turn back of the thumb. There is very little passion of the ordinary sort indicated in the development of the mount of Venus so much towards the angles, and the mount of the Moon will, with the low-set heart line, give her the capacity for loving an ideal, and singular freedom from jealousy.

Her thumb is firm, but the palm is really hollow and shows how much she dislikes contest and struggle, while the many nerve lines show the sensitiveness of the nature.

It is in the lines, however, that the chief interest lies.

The ring of Saturn lies between B¹ marking the commencement, one branch rising upwards towards B², and the other (more faintly indicated) terminating close to a Mercury influence. This signifies misfortune and trouble through the emotions.

C marks an early friendship, cut off by opposition. D¹–D² signifies a short acquaintance, leading to matrimony around the age of twenty-one. Notice how the line where it joins the life seems inclined to star, always a sign of great misfortune through C, after which there is more independence, the line dividing into two for a short time. Now, at this period there was great trouble, and the result was that the subject got a divorce with no difficulty, and the custody of the one child. The or-

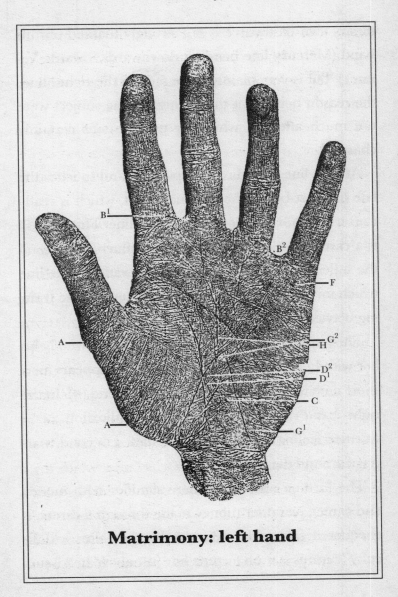

Matrimony: left hand

dinary sign of divorce is not strongly marked on this hand (Mercury line bending downwards towards Venus F), but is very plainly to be seen in the right hand, the reason being that the feelings of the subject were not much affected, while her position was certainly changed.

At G^1 a line rises directly upwards, and touches the fate line just below the line marked H, which is really the termination of another influence line. This line (G^1) is a career line, but starts from an influence line, and the influence and the career form a rather wide line which forks just below G^2, the new influence line H rising between them.

The reading given is that of an old friend who helps her with her career, but whose influence appears for a short time to be displaced by another friend (H). In the right hand this friendship shows indication of a warmer feeling and appears to mark a second marriage around the age of thirty.

The fortune line, which here signifies both money and career, or rather money made through a career, is chequered and varies considerably, but after a difficulty (curious star on fortune line just above head) success seems most probable in spite of drawbacks and troubles (lines crossing the fate line). The squares indicated in the palm of the hand show escapes from danger. The many journey lines on the mount of the Moon indicate travels (the subject was born abroad and is French on her mother's side).

The future for this hand looks certainly brighter than the past.

XX – A Mother

'I'd rather teach twenty the right way to go, than be one of the twenty to follow mine own instructions.'

And of nothing in life can this be said so truly as of the training and management of children. Those who have developed strong opinions on the raising of children may find that in practice their theories are of little benefit. Some charming parents have detestable children, and some of the most unpleasant parents have quite delightful children. Heredity has much to do with this, but education more, just as the finest rose bush neglected runs wile while on a common hedge stake, prunted and budded, we see the finest blossoms.

We cannot expect to find perfection in one individual, but we have taken the print of the hand of a mother who has succeeded in bringing up her children so that they are turning out well, and after all it is by results that we must judge. The thumb is held in, and the mount of the Moon is developed towards the centre of the hand, so that the shape of the hand appears oblong, indicating someone who does not have originality or creative faculty. There is imagination, but its area is limited (B^1–B^2, the boundaries of Mars).

The first finger is straight but rather short, evenly developed and rather blunt. There is a sense of duty and trust but no personal love of power. The long head line and second phalange of the thumb, the firm palm, and first knot on the thumb show that where she is confident of an issue she will assert her authority. The second finger is thick and straight, long enough for prudence but not heavy enough for morbidity. The third finger, from its length, in an inartistic hand, indicates the love of perfection. The fourth finger is rather short, thick and blunt. She will be tactful out of consideration and not from diplomacy.

The lines are on the whole somewhat ordinary. C indicates the rise of the fate line, which, lying as it does away from the life line, would indicate early responsibility. D is an influence line joining the fate line between the ages of twenty-two and twenty-three. E is the

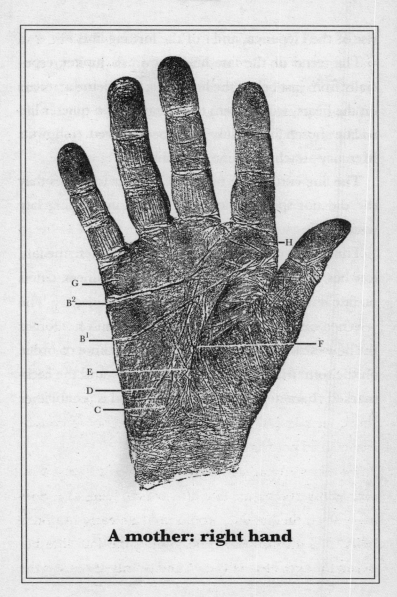

A mother: right hand

rise of the Hepatica, and F of the fortune line.

The trend of the fate line is towards Jupiter, especially from just below the head line, but, being arrested on the heart, would seem to indicate that a quieter life will be chosen for the sake of someone loved. G shows a Mercury attachment line, and only one.

The line cutting the mount of Jupiter indicates that she did not spend much time socialising during her youth.

The square indicated on the head line where the fate touches, may be read as an escape from illness, dated on fate line at about thirty-seven years of age.

When summing up the character, we must not forget the housewifely capacity indicated by the knot of order on the somewhat square-looking fingers; and the most marked characteristic of the whole hand is reliability.

XXI – A Cook

One of the practical uses of palmistry could be to have a logical reason for choice of staff and not to have to learn by painful experience that a short-fingered waiter will damage the crockery and be less than diplomatic with the customers; or that a cook with the same peculiarity, particularly if her palm is thick and heavy, will be oblivious to the finer details of culinary art and trust to fate rather than skill that the result will be eatable.

This subject excels more in the organisation of the kitchen than as a chef – the lower phalanges are sufficiently thick to indicate that she is honest and straightforward. The true chef has the hand of a gourmet, combined with that of an artist, and condescends to nothing but the preparation of food. Here, though, we see the hand of an individual who has succeeded in combining various practical qualities with agood temper – the nails being well formed, pale and rounded at their bases.

The thumb shows obstinacy of will, by its thickness at A–A, with its distinctive curve (B–B) witnessing to the power the emotions have over her actions. The width of the hand signifies the love of fresh air, and its squareness practicality. The well-marked lines show good health and constitution, the separated fingers independence, their length the capacity for detail, the knots the love of order, their pointed tips a love of refinement, and the mount of the Moon being so large, there is an element of romance and idealism in the nature in spite of the very practical short head line, which makes her judgment shrewd and sensible.

D–D shows that the mount of Mercury beneath the fourth finger is good and well developed, and the width, height and firmness of the plain of Mars imply that she can take her own part but loves peace as a rule.

The pointed first finger indicates a love of reading, this formation in the second gives a lack of caution, and with that pointed thumb, and a deep heart line, she should be very careful in her choice of friends or

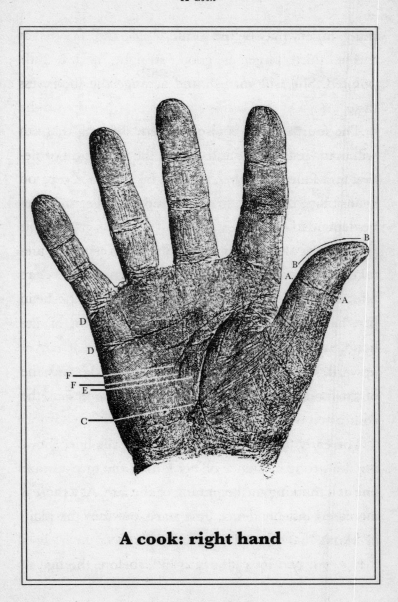

A cook: right hand

much misery may be the result.

The third finger is good, straight, and a little pointed. She will garnish and arrange the food with taste.

The fourth finger is also pointed, showing that she will manage tactfully, and, taking the formation of the first and fourth together, she will be able to accept responsibility, organize, arrange, and manage, and is to be depended on.

The lines are few, but deep. She is not nervous, and takes life very much as it comes. The heart shows deep affection for few people (short, deep line). The head line has the upward curve toward the palm of the hand, which might denote throat delicacy; it curves upward, showing by its tendency towards Mars instead of the mount of the Moon, practical common sense, as contrasted with imaginative judgment.

The early fate line is mixed with the life line, showing the strong influence of her family, the tiny upward line at C marking the beginning of the fate. At E there is increased independence (line starts out into the plain of Mars).

F, F, are two love affairs, a little before the age of

thirty – probably around twenty-seven or twenty-eight. Matrimony is most probable, but the date is not yet fixed.

The formation of the Venus mount makes her kindly and benevolent, and fond of children, and the lines of the mount of Mercury suggest that she would make a good nurse.

The development of the mount of Jupiter will also make her sociable and given to hospitality.

These are the chief points that indicate theat her employer is very fortunate.

XXII – A Commonplace
Subject

This at first glance is an ordinary hand. The fingers are rather long in proportion. He will, therefore, like to be directed by others as they are also somewhat spatulated, but in the left hand the fourth finger and thumb are conic, and this is also the case with the first and thumb (right hand). This gives a mixture of ideas. The first finger pointed indicates a love of reading. The second finger is more separated in the right hand than in the left. It is therefore probable that he has become more independent in ideas, but the finger itself is much the same, fairly long, showing sufficient force of circumstance to keep the subject in something of a groove. The top phalange is fairly long indicating prudence. The long middle phalange signifies a love of flowers. However, the short lower phalange, or rather it is shorter in the right than in the left, shows that he has not pursued an interest in gardening. The great difference existing between the two hands lies in the position of the third finger, which is much stronger in the right than in the left hand. Noting the long 'constructive' tips of the fingers in connection with this 'art' finger, he has probably gone in for mechanics and engineering, including technical drawing and actual construction; while with such a good mount of the Moon his imagination, aided by his power of imitation, may make him ingenious in application.

His fourth finger is a good one, showing that any failure in achievement is due to the fact that his heart is stronger than his head (look at the heart line and contrast). His judgment is impulsive (head line sloping to imagination F^1–F^2); although it probably makes him a more pleasant companion, he is easily turned from his purpose by his emotions. He gives excellent advice to others (B-B) and is very loyal to his friends, particularly if they are in trouble, but he is a little fickle in his admiration (thumb pointed A, second phalange B-B, the lower angle C-C rather short).

We notice that on the life line (D) there is a serious break, which from its position would indicate the age of fourteen. A very serious accident with a cricket ball

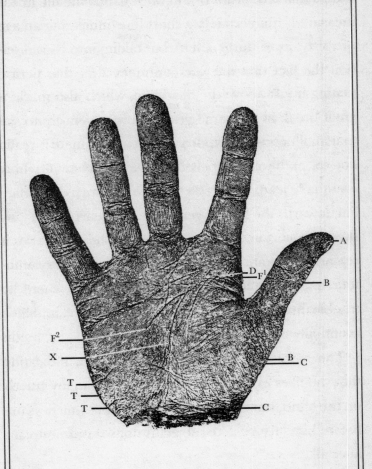

A commonplace subject: right hand

is thus marked. From D-X in both hands the life line is measured. It is certainly a short line (indicating an age of thirty-six to thirty seven), but taking into consideration the fact that the fate continues after that period (dating it just above the head line, which also marks a great break at the same year), we may venture to say that an illness which appears most unfortunate is really not so, as he is compelled to make a change which eventually leads to success (observe the turn of the fate line towards the first finger above the heart line). F^1, F^2, show the start and termination of the head line. G is a remarkable point in the life (about the age of twenty-four on all the lines), and is marked everywhere by trouble (broken and crossed heart, head, fate, and life), eventually overcome but never forgotten.

The hand is hard and flat, which is an indication that he likes exercise, and there are not many travels on the hand, but two or three momentous journeys are before him (T,T,T). The subject is not so commonplace after all.

XXIII – A Mad Subject

This study is very interesting, and especially so when you understand the extreme difficulty of persuading so restless a subject to remain quiet during the process of 'casting'. The value of an accurate print of such hands is very great, especially as this enables us to compare the progress the disease has made by the comparison of the two hands.

Notice first the network of lines which indicates the extremely nervous temperament, and secondly, the want of proportion in the lines. All are of nearly the same width and depth, yet so tangled and broken up that it is evident there is no power of concentration, but that everything, however trivial, is for the moment of supreme importance.

It is not so much in the lines themselves that we look for indications of brain disease, but in the outline of the hand.

All the right-hand fingertips show more of a clubbed tendency than in the left hand. The thumb, especially in the left hand, is not abnormal, showing simply weakness of the will (tapering end), and its stretch is not remarkable. In the right hand, however, the thumb is placed much nearer the first finger, and the tip is thicker, while the centre is waisted and almost appears shorter. It signifies the gratification of the will at any cost.

All the fingers are thickened in the right hand, and the difference in the outline of the palm of the hand is most marked. In the left hand we notice the slight narrowness across the palm just below the bases of the fingers, which indicates hysteria, the absence of the mounts of Mars, Mercury and the Moon, the great development of Venus, the weak thumb, and the good heart line. This is the type of hand that so largely prevails in the type of person that often errs and suffers through excess of emotion.

In the right hand there is a marked change – the hand is larger, Mercury and Mars are more than ever conspicuous by their absence, and the curious bulge (right hand, A-A) marks an extraordinary develop-

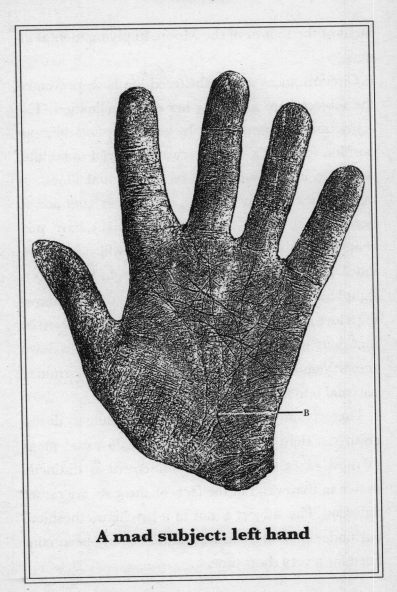

A mad subject: left hand

ment of the mount of the Moon, implying mental illness.

Circumstances and a sheltered life have prevented the subject from gratifying her early inclination. The restrictions imposed on her by her family and their opposition to a lover, who afterwards proved unfaithful, were the immediate cause of her mental illness. A more judicious early training, and stricter attention to her physical health and wellbeing might have prevented much of this, as any student will notice how much better the left hand is than the right hand. (At B, right hand and left hand, a line rises to the fate, showing a love affair at about the age of eighteen, crossed by a curious line running from the base of logic down across Venus, life, and fate, and showing determined parental opposition.)

There is only one small square, difficult to distinguish (C-C right hand), which may puzzle a student, as in most cases the idea of confinement is distinctly shown in that way, but the facts of this case are rather different. The subject is not in a psychiatric hospital, but under private treatment, and has only been confined for a very short time.

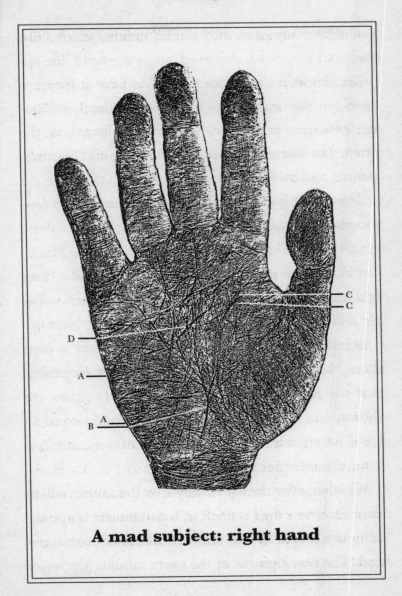

A mad subject: right hand

Unlike many cases of a similar nature, which show the heart line much shattered, while the head line appears almost normal, this print shows for at least ten years (on the head line) a long broken island, indicating extreme nervous prostration and disease of the brain, but later on in life the line certainly becomes clearer, and may indicate improvement.

The heart line is curiously placed, unusually low, showing with so large a development of Venus that the gratification of the emotions is the main aim in life.

The life line is much broken up, with many crosses and small down-dropping lines. Her constitution is feeble and she is always ailing.

She thinks a great deal about money, and is constantly brooding over expense, so it is not surprising that the fortune line is much marked. Legacies are shown, one especially (D, right hand) should come to her if it were not for the interposition of a relative (line from Venus cutting off fortune line).

Whether, after the age of fifty-five, the subject will to some extent recover, is unclear, but that there is a possibility is justified by the uncrossed lines after that period. The development of the lower mounts (the lower nature) and the absence of calculation (head line), control (Mars), and reason (second phalange of thumb 'waisted') lay the subject at the mercy of violent gusts of passion, perhaps leading to agressive tendencies.

The lines on the mount of the Moon are voyages taken for health. The innumerable crossed lines cannot be separately read as they appear and disappear, according to the subject's state of health.

XXIV – A Circus Rider

As a type, this hand at first sight seems ordinary and commonplace to a degree, but his occupation would seem to prove otherwise. This hand is an effective contrast to the supersensitive mystic (*see* page 195).

Any lover of animals would have been curious to find out the secret by which such perfect control is gained over a horse. He has perfect control over his animals and remarkable athletic power leaping from the ground on to the bare back of the horse galloping round the ring. In the 'act' with 'Little Lizzie' (*see* A child circus rider, page 251), who is his daughter, both father and child seem scarcely ordinary mortals, so much at home do they seem in midair!

Away from his usual surroundings the subject seems quiet, reserved and taciturn, and this is indicated by the second finger being in reality heavier than it appears on the print, and both mounts of Mars and the plain being very firm and heavy. The fourth finger shows capacity, but its low setting and the somewhat shortened first finger will lead him to dislike any undue responsibility. The love of detail (fingers really longer than the palm), and artistic perfection (long straight third finger), will lead him to do everything he undertakes with the greatest thoroughness. Plucky (high mount Mars under Mercury) and prompt, he has great self-control and presence of mind, and should a fall seem certain, he can turn a half-somersault or otherwise save his neck.

He is an especially interesting subject as an animal-trainer. The large and well-developed mount of the Moon shows that he could never ill-treat an animal, and the faculty of concentration shown in the head line (deep and well marked) indicates his entire absorption in the business of the moment, while the firm, reasonable thumb, with its long middle phalange, shows that he would not be unreasonable in his demands.

The curving tip does not contradict the force of will shown otherwise. It simply indicates that he *can* yield, and redeems the character from what might be unreasonable obstinacy. He is warm-hearted (good heart

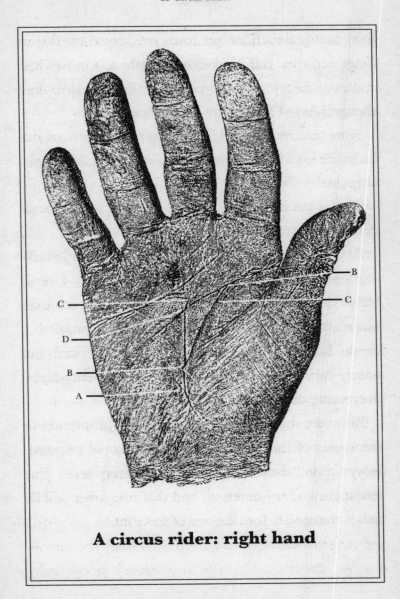

A circus rider: right hand

line), not jealous (line set low), strongly conservative (fingers rather stiff and close together), fond of the country (heavy middle phalange of Saturn), and though fond of fishing, he hates the sea.

Note that he has little imagination and does not suffer in the least from nerves (the mount of the Moon not large, palm unlined).

At A is the broken star which marks a serious accident at seventeen.

At B, the fate line and life line, we see a break, marking a severe attack of typhoid fever. A small, fading, bluish dent shows the nature of the illness, which took place at twenty-four. There is a curious little mark at C on the life line, almost imperceptible in the print, but which indicates an injury to the knee at twenty-eight, preventing his work for fourteen months.

Palmistry shows that he will become a proprietor, or something of the sort, involving a position of responsibility around the age of thirty-six or thirty-seven (line tending towards Jupiter, D), and that his career will be much changed before the age of forty (C).

XXV – A Child Circus Rider

It is rather a disputed point how definitely the exact progress of events can be told by looking at a child's hand, but about the characteristics there is no doubt whatever. As the future oak is contained in the acorn, so in the child's hand are all the characteristics that will develop into personality.

Anyone who saw 'Little Lizzie' walking up and down stairs on her hands, her feet dangling over her back; standing on two chairs, and then, turning backward, picking up a coin with her lips; rolling like a wheel, with her face outwards, in and out of the ring with an air of indifference, looking far cooler than the audience felt, on that blazing day beneath the circus roof, must have wondered at the courage, pluck, and endurance that made such a performance possible. A smiling little thing of about thirteen, with short curled hair and big blue eyes, she rode the barebacked pony with perfection and the pony's total confidence. It is no surprise then to see the development of the mount beneath the third finger (Apollo) to which palmists assign the quality of mercy and love of animals.

Her little hands are wonderfully free from the small nerve lines that distinguish some other little subjects. She is not impressionable, although the outline of the hand is refined, the fingers being of medium length and somewhat conic; the third and fourth (left hand) differ somewhat, being slightly spatulate.

The palm is flat, and the mounts of Mars are well placed and hard, showing pluck and the power of endurance. The thumb shows a firm will, but by its curved tip she is easily led through the emotions; the second phalange shows that she can look at a subject from all sides, and the observation shown on the length of the head line in connection with the aforementioned Mars plain and mounts gives her forethought and quickness in emergencies. She has little imagination, and is not in the least apprehensive; trouble comes, but she does not worry about it beforehand, and the cheerful buoyancy of her nature shown by the development of the mount of Mercury (beneath the fourth finger)

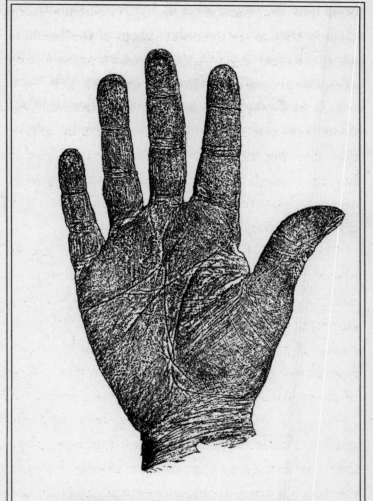

A child circus rider: right hand

shows how she would meet it. She is affectionate and warm-hearted, and responds easily to sympathy; naturally quick and full of life, there are great capacities for organization and management beneath that curly crop. If to do one thing well makes life worth living, you need not desire 'Little Lizzie' to change her profession for a more ordinary schoolgirl life.

XXVI – A Hypnotist

The practice of hypnosis or hypnotic suggestion, has been known from the earliest ages, but is no longer classed among occult practices.

One of the first attempts to render some use from the phenomenon was made by the Austrian physician Franz Anton Mesmer (1734-1815) who believed the human nervous system to be magnetized just as the earth is. He called this force 'animal magnetism'. The therapy he devised involved the use of iron magnets and the laying on of hands. He would stare fixedly into the patient's eyes, slowly waving his hands or a magic wand in front of the patient, which caused a hypnotic state. Any use derived from the treatment was attributed to the magnets. Hypnosis is now an integral practice in psychoanalysis – for example in the treatment of hysterical, and compulsive disorders – thanks to the work of Jean Martin Charcot (1825–1893), Josef

Breuer (1842–1925) and, most famously Sigmund Freud (1856–1939).

This is the print of the hand of one who makes his living from the use of hypnosis as a means of entertainment. He has given many public displays of his capacity for inducing the hypnotic state in others, and was himself anxious to be buried for three weeks while in a trance condition, which, however, the American authorities refused to allow.

This subject, like others with hypnotic powers, typically shows a developed Moon mount towards Mars. In this instance, the double line of fortune, one rising from the life and the other from the fate (A^1-A^2), might be explained as denoting a highly unusual aptitude in the subject.

The extraordinary length of the second finger in our subject gives the tendency to fatalism. The unusual barring of the head and heart lines (which almost make them appear as if barring the hand) indicates the development of logic, and the presence of the philosophic knot, with the high flat palm, give him the capacity for resistance, the power of calculation, and the capacity for foresight.

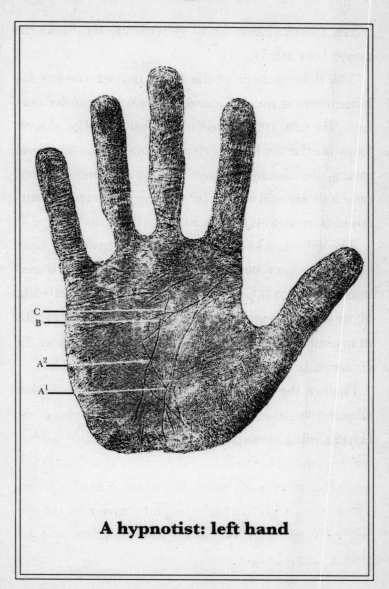

A hypnotist: left hand

His fourth finger shows general capacity and the power over others.

The development of the lower part of the hand is large; there is much force of passion held under control. 'He who rules himself rules others'. The double rings on the fourth finger are remarkable, the lower giving the lowest phalange the appearance of being only half an inch long. The reading for this peculiarity could be mistaken judgment in material things.

The fate line lying deeply marked up to the head line and fainter beyond indicates a period of uncertainty between the ages of thirty-three and thirty-four (B) or thirty-six and thirty-eight (C), followed later by many changes owing to health (the long break in the centre of the head line indicates a nervous illness).

Further, the line stopping on the heart indicates that emotion so long kept under control may prove too commanding, and spoil a fine career.

XXVII – A Study in Lines

The accompanying prints have been selected for the somewhat curious arrangement of the lines, and also for the very marked differences in the hands. The character is an impulsive one, but there is more caution than appears on the conical finger of Saturn, the finger being much more spatulated, as the left side of the first phalange is flattened from the pressure of the pen. Her affections are warm (good heart line), her emotions calm and more often excited through melody, the beautiful, and the ideal than in the ordinary channels (mount Venus is flat except towards the angles, and the Moon high and hard). Notice the length of the thumb from tip to base. It is strong and every phalange developed. The first and second are of equal length, the latter being singularly square and evenly developed, while the former is very firm and curves a little outward, showing that the will is decided, but yields in trifles, and is subject to the control of the reason and logic, even in the emotions (heart and head lines of equal length).

The imagination is very much used, the plain is fairly high, both mounts of Mars are well placed and firm, and the mount Mercury is high and hard. There is, therefore, no shrinking from contest, but much control, and a sense of humour will prevent her from making herself aggressive.

The Jupiter finger is insignificant, which is curious, as her powers of organization are good. She has always had to arrange and manage for others, and has, on the whole, been remarkably successful.

One reading of this peculiarity is that she had no desire of personal rule, and much preferred being let alone to live her own life, but that circumstances having placed her in the position, the energy, promptitude and decision of character made her take the lead. With a change of circumstances, she would be more than willing to forego responsibility. The curve of the same finger is in the second and third phalanges, and shows a disposition to morbid pride. Had the first phalange appeared conspicuously curved, there would have

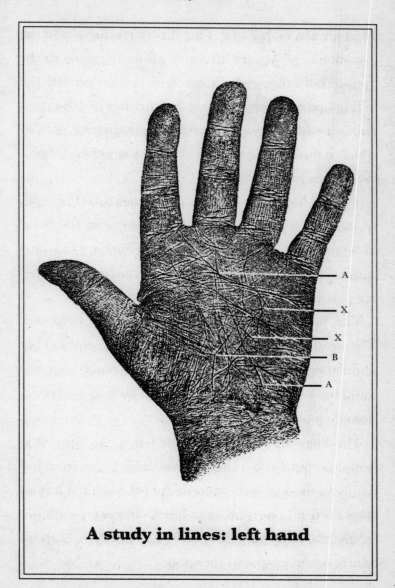

A

X

X

B

A

A study in lines: left hand

been a want of honour. This short first finger and the low mount of Jupiter also give an indifference to the opinions of others, which, taken in connection with the falling-apart fingers, shows independence of character, and with Mercury developed, an acceptance of that which is disagreeable yet inevitable, and a cheerful philosophy as to good results.

The left hand shows many more lines than the right, which would indicate difficulties overcome, the main idea (shown by the ascending and deepening fate line) causing her to take but little notice of impediments, being absorbed in the idea of her career.

The heart line shows inherited physical weakness. The head line is curiously divided into two parallel but undulating lines – the reading given being that the mind has two interests, running side by side, and occasionally interfering with each other.

The lines marked A, A, on the left hand, show that from quite early days she has lived a life apart from her family in thought and interest, even though she has always lived at home and been much connected with her family (the right hand fate line). The line A, A, on both hands, deserves special mention.

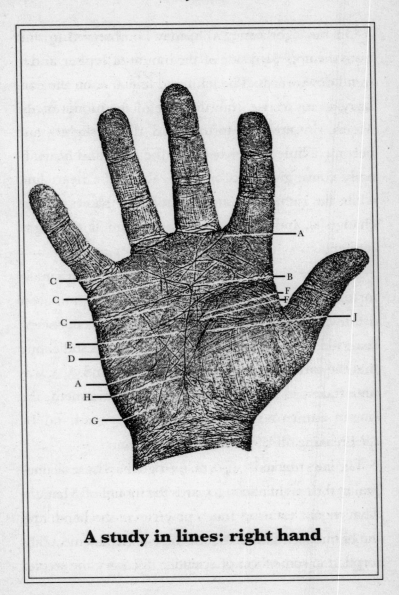

A study in lines: right hand

On the right hand, A, A, may be observed to start from the upper left side of the mount of Jupiter, and to trend downwards. The left hand line A, A, on the contrary, seems to rise from the base of the mount of the Moon, rise upwards to the head, divide slightly, and become a little fainter between the head and heart, finally converging into one line above the heart line, while the right hand at the same date shows a great change (B), and improvement in position (line rising to Jupiter).

Now, the line A, A, on the right hand, originally formed part of the ring of Saturn, but began to grow downwards when the subject was about twenty-seven years old, and has visibly continued to do so, indicating that the career is marked out on the left hand. A, A, was undertaken in consequence of a disappointment, the ring of Saturn being much broken up (right hand) by the breaking off of the line.

The lines marked C, C, C, on the right hand, are all unusual in their termination towards the mount of Mercury. That mount exercises much power over the hand, and the distinct bend towards it of these lines may mean absorption in some form of scientific discovery, the second knots (love of investigation and research) being developed.

The point marked B, left hand, shows the rise of the fortune line at about the age of nineteen, when the subject began to earn money for herself.

In the right hand, D shows the career line and fortune line starting almost together, and forming a kind of loop, indicating that it and some individual hobby, that makes money, start together.

The odd little line marked E, right hand, at its starting point shows some outside interest, taken up through the influence of a friend (short influence line starting the line), and F, F, indicate two fresh interests.

The apparent island on the left hand (marked X, X) at its start and termination, is only a mixture of a waved Hepatica and the presentiment line. The Hepatica in the right hand is good on the whole, if a little wavy and uncertain to start with. G, right hand, is the beginning of the fortune line. There have been many influences in the life, and marriage has been intended twice; once at the age of twenty-two (H, right hand), and again at thirty to thirty-one, where a very faint influence line may be discerned just below the point E on the right hand. Matrimony itself is late in life, about thirty-seven, and is indicated at J on the right hand by an influence line inside the life line, touching that line with a sort of square.

The second phalange of the thumb is lined and shows opposition from the family to two plans (two lines).

The crosses on the mount of Jupiter show two gratified ambitions.

There are many journeys, short and long, shown by the lines on the mount of the Moon.

Appendix: Putting Theory into Practice

The following pages have been set aside for you to record the notable features of the palms of yourself, friends and family. There is space on the palm outlines to record the features of the lines, fingers and mounts and there is also space provided for you to make a note of these findings and to make your own interpretations of the features. Use the first section of the book to help you to find the lines and their features and use the latter section of Life Studies to see how an experienced palmist interprets these features.

Remember that a good palmist never alarms his or her subjects with sweeping negative statements about possible life events. For example, no serious palmist would ever consider making a speculation about the age at which death occurs. Do not use your new skills irresponsibly.

Name of subject: _____

The Hand's Physical Features – Chirognomy

Size of hands and fingers: _____

Colour: _____

Skin texture: _____

Shape: _____

Hand type: _____

Fingernails: _____

Interpretation: _____

_____

Features of The Fingers and Mounts of the Hand

Jupiter: _____

Saturn: _____

Apollo: _____

Mercury: _____

Venus: _____

Mars: _____

Moon: _____

The plain of Mars: _____

Interpretation: _____

_____

_____

Features of the Lines of the Palm – Chiromancy

Line of life: _____

Line of head: _____

Line of heart: _____

Line of fate/destiny: _____

Line of fortune: _____

Line of intuition: _____

Line of business & health: _____

Girdle of Venus: _____

Lines of affection: _____

Bracelets: _____

The Great Triangle (of head, life and fate lines): _____

_____

Interpretation: _____

_____

_____

_____

_____

LEFT HAND – FATED THINGS:
NOTABLE FEATURES

RIGHT HAND – FREE WILL:
NOTABLE FEATURES

COMPARISON OF LEFT AND RIGHT HANDS:

ANALYSIS OF THE READING:

NAME OF SUBJECT: _____

THE HAND'S PHYSICAL FEATURES – CHIROGNOMY
Size of hands and fingers: _____
Colour: _____
Skin texture: _____
Shape: _____
Hand type: _____
Fingernails: _____
Interpretation: _____

_____

FEATURES OF THE FINGERS AND MOUNTS OF THE HAND
Jupiter: _____
Saturn: _____
Apollo: _____
Mercury: _____
Venus: _____
Mars: _____
Moon: _____
The plain of Mars: _____
Interpretation: _____

_____

_____

FEATURES OF THE LINES OF THE PALM – CHIROMANCY
Line of life: _____
Line of head: _____
Line of heart: _____
Line of fate/destiny: _____
Line of fortune: _____
Line of intuition: _____
Line of business & health: _____
Girdle of Venus: _____
Lines of affection: _____
Bracelets: _____
The Great Triangle (of head, life and fate lines): _____

_____

Interpretation: _____

_____

_____

_____

_____

LEFT HAND – FATED THINGS:
NOTABLE FEATURES

RIGHT HAND – FREE WILL:
NOTABLE FEATURES

_____
_____
_____
_____
_____

COMPARISON OF LEFT AND RIGHT HANDS:

_____
_____
_____
_____
_____

ANALYSIS OF THE READING:

_____
_____
_____
_____
_____
_____

NAME OF SUBJECT: _____

THE HAND'S PHYSICAL FEATURES – CHIROGNOMY
Size of hands and fingers: _____
Colour: _____
Skin texture: _____
Shape: _____
Palm type: _____
Interpretation: _____
_____
_____

FEATURES OF THE FINGERS AND MOUNTS OF THE HAND
Jupiter: _____
Saturn: _____
Apollo: _____
Mercury: _____
Venus: _____
Mars: _____
Moon: _____
The plain of Mars: _____
Interpretation: _____
_____
_____

FEATURES OF THE LINES OF THE PALM – CHIROMANCY
Line of life: _____
Line of head: _____
Line of heart: _____
Line of fate/destiny: _____
Line of fortune: _____
Line of intuition: _____
Line of business & health: _____
Girdle of Venus: _____
Lines of affection: _____
Bracelets: _____
The Great Triangle (of head, life and fate lines): _____
_____
Interpretation: _____
_____
_____
_____
_____

LEFT HAND – FATED THINGS:
NOTABLE FEATURES

RIGHT HAND – FREE WILL:
NOTABLE FEATURES

_____

_____

_____

_____

_____

COMPARISON OF LEFT AND RIGHT HANDS:

ANALYSIS OF THE READING:

273

NAME OF SUBJECT: _____

THE HAND'S PHYSICAL FEATURES – CHIROGNOMY
Size of hands and fingers: _____
Colour: _____
Skin texture: _____
Shape: _____
Palm type: _____
Interpretation: _____
_____
_____

FEATURES OF THE FINGERS AND MOUNTS OF THE HAND
Jupiter: _____
Saturn: _____
Apollo: _____
Mercury: _____
Venus: _____
Mars: _____
Moon: _____
The plain of Mars: _____
Interpretation: _____
_____
_____

FEATURES OF THE LINES OF THE PALM – CHIROMANCY
Line of life: _____
Line of head: _____
Line of heart: _____
Line of fate/destiny: _____
Line of fortune: _____
Line of intuition: _____
Line of business & health: _____
Girdle of Venus: _____
Lines of affection: _____
Bracelets: _____
The Great Triangle (of head, life and fate lines): _____
_____
Interpretation: _____
_____
_____
_____
_____

LEFT HAND – FATED THINGS:
NOTABLE FEATURES

_____
_____
_____
_____
_____

RIGHT HAND – FREE WILL:
NOTABLE FEATURES

_____
_____
_____
_____
_____

COMPARISON OF LEFT AND RGHT HANDS:

_____
_____
_____
_____
_____

ANALYSIS OF THE READING:

_____
_____
_____
_____
_____
_____

NAME OF SUBJECT: _____

THE HAND'S PHYSICAL FEATURES – CHIROGNOMY

Size of hands and fingers: _____
Colour: _____
Skin texture: _____
Shape: _____
Palm type: _____
Interpretation: _____
_____
_____

FEATURES OF THE FINGERS AND MOUNTS OF THE HAND

Jupiter: _____
Saturn: _____
Apollo: _____
Mercury: _____
Venus: _____
Mars: _____
Moon: _____
The plain of Mars: _____
Interpretation: _____
_____
_____

FEATURES OF THE LINES OF THE PALM – CHIROMANCY

Line of life: _____
Line of head: _____
Line of heart: _____
Line of fate/destiny: _____
Line of fortune: _____
Line of intuition: _____
Line of business & health: _____
Girdle of Venus: _____
Lines of affection: _____
Bracelets: _____
The Great Triangle (of head, life and fate lines): _____
_____

Interpretation: _____
_____
_____
_____
_____

LEFT HAND – FATED THINGS:
NOTABLE FEATURES

_____
_____
_____
_____
_____

RIGHT HAND – FREE WILL:
NOTABLE FEATURES

_____
_____
_____
_____
_____

COMPARISON OF LEFT AND RIGHT HANDS:

_____
_____
_____
_____
_____

ANALYSIS OF THE READING:

_____
_____
_____
_____
_____
_____

NAME OF SUBJECT: _____

THE HAND'S PHYSICAL FEATURES – CHIROGNOMY
Size of hands and fingers: _____
Colour: _____
Skin texture: _____
Shape: _____
Palm type: _____
Interpretation: _____
_____
_____

FEATURES OF THE FINGERS AND MOUNTS OF THE HAND
Jupiter: _____
Saturn: _____
Apollo: _____
Mercury: _____
Venus: _____
Mars: _____
Moon: _____
The plain of Mars: _____
Interpretation: _____
_____
_____

FEATURES OF THE LINES OF THE PALM – CHIROMANCY
Line of life: _____
Line of head: _____
Line of heart: _____
Line of fate/destiny: _____
Line of fortune: _____
Line of intuition: _____
Line of business & health: _____
Girdle of Venus: _____
Lines of affection: _____
Bracelets: _____
The Great Triangle (of head, life and fate lines): _____
_____

Interpretation: _____
_____
_____
_____
_____

Appendix: Putting Theory into Practice

LEFT HAND – FATED THINGS:
NOTABLE FEATURES

RIGHT HAND – FREE WILL:
NOTABLE FEATURES

_____
_____
_____
_____
_____

COMPARISON OF LEFT AND RIGHT HANDS:
_____
_____
_____
_____

ANALYSIS OF THE READING:
_____
_____
_____
_____
_____

NAME OF SUBJECT: _____

THE HAND'S PHYSICAL FEATURES – CHIROGNOMY

Size of hands and fingers: _____
Colour: _____
Skin texture: _____
Shape: _____
Palm type: _____
Interpretation: _____
_____
_____

FEATURES OF THE FINGERS AND MOUNTS OF THE HAND

Jupiter: _____
Saturn: _____
Apollo: _____
Mercury: _____
Venus: _____
Mars: _____
Moon: _____
The plain of Mars: _____
Interpretation: _____
_____
_____

FEATURES OF THE LINES OF THE PALM – CHIROMANCY

Line of life: _____
Line of head: _____
Line of heart: _____
Line of fate/destiny: _____
Line of fortune: _____
Line of intuition: _____
Line of business & health: _____
Girdle of Venus: _____
Lines of affection: _____
Bracelets: _____
The Great Triangle (of head, life and fate lines): _____
_____

Interpretation: _____
_____
_____
_____
_____

LEFT HAND – FATED THINGS:
NOTABLE FEATURES

RIGHT HAND – FREE WILL:
NOTABLE FEATURES

_____
_____
_____
_____
_____

COMPARISON OF LEFT AND RIGHT HANDS:
_____
_____
_____
_____
_____

ANALYSIS OF THE READING:
_____
_____
_____
_____
_____

NAME OF SUBJECT: _____

THE HAND'S PHYSICAL FEATURES – CHIROGNOMY
Size of hands and fingers: _____
Colour: _____
Skin texture: _____
Shape: _____
Palm type: _____
Interpretation: _____
_____
_____
_____

FEATURES OF THE FINGERS AND MOUNTS OF THE HAND
Jupiter: _____
Saturn: _____
Apollo: _____
Mercury: _____
Venus: _____
Mars: _____
Moon: _____
The plain of Mars: _____
Interpretation: _____
_____
_____

FEATURES OF THE LINES OF THE PALM – CHIROMANCY
Line of life: _____
Line of head: _____
Line of heart: _____
Line of fate/destiny: _____
Line of fortune: _____
Line of intuition: _____
Line of business & health: _____
Girdle of Venus: _____
Lines of affection: _____
Bracelets: _____
The Great Triangle (of head, life and fate lines): _____
_____

Interpretation: _____
_____
_____
_____
_____

LEFT HAND – FATED THINGS:
NOTABLE FEATURES

_____
_____
_____
_____
_____

RIGHT HAND – FREE WILL:
NOTABLE FEATURES

_____
_____
_____
_____
_____

COMPARISON OF LEFT AND RIGHT HANDS:

_____
_____
_____
_____
_____

ANALYSIS OF THE READING:

_____
_____
_____
_____
_____
_____

NAME OF SUBJECT: _____

THE HAND'S PHYSICAL FEATURES – CHIROGNOMY
Size of hands and fingers: _____
Colour: _____
Skin texture: _____
Shape: _____
Palm type: _____
Interpretation: _____
_____
_____

FEATURES OF THE FINGERS AND MOUNTS OF THE HAND
Jupiter: _____
Saturn: _____
Apollo: _____
Mercury: _____
Venus: _____
Mars: _____
Moon: _____
The plain of Mars: _____
Interpretation: _____
_____
_____

FEATURES OF THE LINES OF THE PALM – CHIROMANCY
Line of life: _____
Line of head: _____
Line of heart: _____
Line of fate/destiny: _____
Line of fortune: _____
Line of intuition: _____
Line of business & health: _____
Girdle of Venus: _____
Lines of affection: _____
Bracelets: _____
The Great Triangle (of head, life and fate lines): _____
_____

Interpretation: _____
_____
_____
_____
_____

LEFT HAND – FATED THINGS:
NOTABLE FEATURES

RIGHT HAND – FREE WILL:
NOTABLE FEATURES

_____
_____
_____
_____
_____

   _____
   _____
   _____
   _____
   _____

COMPARISON OF LEFT AND RIGHT HANDS:

_____
_____
_____
_____

ANALYSIS OF THE READING:

_____
_____
_____
_____
_____

NAME OF SUBJECT: _____

THE HAND'S PHYSICAL FEATURES – CHIROGNOMY

Size of hands and fingers: _____
Colour: _____
Skin texture: _____
Shape: _____
Palm type: _____
Interpretation: _____
_____
_____

FEATURES OF THE FINGERS AND MOUNTS OF THE HAND

Jupiter: _____
Saturn: _____
Apollo: _____
Mercury: _____
Venus: _____
Mars: _____
Moon: _____
The plain of Mars: _____
Interpretation: _____
_____
_____

FEATURES OF THE LINES OF THE PALM – CHIROMANCY

Line of life: _____
Line of head: _____
Line of heart: _____
Line of fate/destiny: _____
Line of fortune: _____
Line of intuition: _____
Line of business & health: _____
Girdle of Venus: _____
Lines of affection: _____
Bracelets: _____
The Great Triangle (of head, life and fate lines): _____
_____

Interpretation: _____
_____
_____
_____
_____

LEFT HAND – FATED THINGS:
NOTABLE FEATURES

RIGHT HAND – FREE WILL:
NOTABLE FEATURES

COMPARISON OF LEFT AND RIGHT HANDS:

ANALYSIS OF THE READING: